The Canadian Press

CAPS and
SPELLING

17th edition
Fully revised and updated

40th anniversary edition

Patti Tasko, Editor

The Canadian Press
The Last Word. First.

36 King St. East, Toronto, Ontario M5C 2L9
www.cp.org

Library and Archives Canada Cataloguing in Publication

CP caps and spelling. -- 17th ed.

Edited by Patti Tasko.

At head of title: The Canadian Press.

ISBN 0-920009-34-4

1. English language--Capitalization. 2. English language--
Orthography and spelling. I. Tasko, Patti II. Canadian
Press

III. Title: Caps and spelling.

PE1450.C72 2005   423'.1   C2005-903883-7

First printing 1965 Revised 1969, 1973, 1976, 1978, 1981,
1985, 1986, 1987, 1988, 1990, 1992, 1996, 1998, 2000, 2003
and 2005.

Copyright 2005 by The Canadian Press

Design and cover art by
Sean Vokey
The Canadian Press

Foreword

Welcome to the 17th edition of *Caps and Spelling!*

This update marks the 40th anniversary of a book that has become an essential reference for people who work with words across Canada.

The goal of the first edition in 1965 – a 46-page pamphlet – was to bring together the proper names and abbreviations most likely to cause problems for those handling copy in Canadian newsrooms. Over the years the listings have expanded, and there are now more than 200 pages of words that prove troublesome to writers and editors of all stripes.

Many of the changes and additions to *Caps and Spelling* come at the request of the writers and editors who use the *CP Stylebook* and this book. Thanks go to those alert and loyal users who help keep this reference up to date, especially CP's Mike Fuhrmann, who has the challenging job of doing the final edit.

Consistency is an editor's good friend, so The Canadian Press tries to keep style changes to a minimum. But when the common usage of words changes, CP style must change too.

Here are some changes in this edition:

• We are moving to paralyze and analyze from paralyse and analyse to reflect the much more common usage of the former.

• N.L. is the new abbreviation for Newfoundland and Labrador, replacing Nfld. This is the preferred abbreviation that has emerged in the province since its name was officially recognized as Newfoundland and Labrador in 2001.

•Proper names of schools are now always capitalized: Leaside High School. Otherwise, it is

Foreword

lowercase: Royal York Academy *(proper name)* but Royal York high school.

•Art styles and schools are now lowercase unless the word is derived from a proper noun or can be confused with a common word: art deco *but* Gothic.

• New listings include: adrenalin, a.k.a., arm's-length, Art, backyard, back road, backup, baroque, bioterrorism, BlackBerry, bullmastiff, burka, Cancon, CEO, chargeback, Companies' Creditors Arrangement Act, concertgoer, Conn Smythe Trophy, databank, diehard, Father, Fefe Dobson, Damhnait Doyle, Atom Egoyan, fuck, gigabyte, global positioning system, Google, hijab, hip hop, homebuyer, IPod, ITunes, karaoke, Kazaa, kilobyte, Kyoto Protocol, Ann-Marie MacDonald, mad cow disease, Mase, MC, Reba McEntire, mulatto, Nickelback, non-fiction, non-stick, Nunatsiavut, PDA, PIN, pleaded, Post-it, poutine, proactive, Quonset, racehorse, ringtone, Rottweiler, run-up, Shariah, shiva, tarsands, T-cell, trans fat, Tube, Turin, Type 1 diabetes, voice-over-Internet protocol, Deryck Whibley, whistleblower, Wi-Fi, Xbox and 9-11.

•Changed listings include: airbag, ballpark, ballplayer, checkerboard, onto (all now one word); CT scan (from CAT); Guinness World Records (changed name), Oxfam Canada, 20th Century Fox (dropped hyphens), Louis St-Laurent (from Saint-Laurent); Seafarers International Union of Canada (dropped apostrophe); 20-something (from twentysomething.

Patti Tasko, Editor   ptasko@cp.org

Capitalization

1. The Canadian Press follows a modified down style. This is the basic rule:
   Capitalize all proper names, the names of departments and agencies of national and provincial governments, trade names, names of associations, companies, clubs, religions, languages, races, places, addresses. Otherwise, lowercase is favoured where a reasonable option exists.

2. Common nouns — church, league — are capitalized when part of a proper name: Anglican Church, National Hockey League. They are normally lowercased when standing alone: the church's stand, a league spokesman.

3. The common-noun elements of proper nouns are normally lowercase in plural uses: the United and Anglican churches, the National and American leagues.

4. Formal titles directly preceding a name are capitalized: Prime Minister Jean Chrétien, Archbishop Aloysius Ambrozic. They are lowercased standing alone and in plural uses: the prime minister, the archbishop, premiers Jean Charest and Ralph Klein.

5. As a rule of thumb, formal titles are those that are almost an integral part of a person's name — they could be used with the surname alone, if that were CP style: Ald. Cowan, Rabbi Steinberg, Sgt. Duplessis.

6. Job descriptions are lowercased: soprano Maria Stratas, managing editor Anne Davies, Acme Corp. chairman Joseph Schultz.

7. Long or cumbersome titles and job descriptions should be set off with commas: Jean Dubois,

energy, mines and resources minister, attended. Or: The energy, mines and resources minister, Jean Dubois, attended. An internationally known Canadian architect, Arthur Erickson, was present.

8. All references to the current Pope, Canada's reigning monarch and the current Governor General are capitalized.

9. Titles of nobility, religion and suchlike that are commonly used instead of the personal name are capitalized: Duke of Kent, Anglican Primate of Canada. But the duke, the primate.

10. The names of national legislative bodies, including some short forms, are capitalized: House of Commons, the House, the Commons; U.S. Senate; Knesset. Provincial legislatures and local councils are lowercased: Quebec national assembly, Toronto city council.

11. National and provincial government departments and agencies are capitalized: Health Canada, Defence Department, Ministry of Natural Resources, U.S. Secret Service. Local government departments and boards are lowercased: parks and property department, Halifax welfare department.

12. Upper courts are capitalized: B.C. Supreme Court, Appeal Court. Lower courts are lowercased: juvenile court, magistrate's court.

13. Canada's military forces are capitalized: Canadian Forces, the Forces. For other forces, army, navy and air force are lowercased when preceded by the name of the country: the Greek air force, the U.S. army. This style is intended for consistency since the proper name is not always a combination of country and force: the

Royal Navy, the British navy; the Royal Air Force, the British air force.

14. Historical periods, historic events, holy days and other special times are capitalized: Middle Ages, First World War, Prohibition, Christmas Eve, Ramadan, Earth Day, October Crisis.

15. Specific geographical regions and features are capitalized: Western Canada, Far North, Lake Superior, Niagara Peninsula. But northern, southern, eastern and western in terms derived from regions are lowercased: a western Canadian, a southerner, northern customs.

16. Regions not generally known as specific geographical areas are lowercase: southern Ontario, eastern Alberta, northern Newfoundland.

17. Sacred names and the proper names and nicknames of the devil are capitalized: the Almighty, Redeemer, Holy Spirit, Allah, Mother of God, Vishnu, Beelzebub, Father of Lies. But devil, hell and heaven are lowercased.

18. Names of races, nations and the like are capitalized: Aboriginal Peoples, Asian, Arab, French-Canadian. But white and black are lowercased.

19. The principal words of titles of books, plays, movies, paintings and the like are capitalized: *A Dictionary of Usage and Style, Androcles and the Lion, Gone With the Wind, Isle of the Dead.* Principal words are nouns, pronouns, adjectives, adverbs, verbs, the first and last word of the title, as well as prepositions and conjunctions of four letters or more. For infinitives, use to Go, to Be. Both words of

Capitalization

compound adjectives are capitalized: Well-Meaning.

20. Nicknames and fanciful names are capitalized: Speedy Gonzales, Mack the Knife, Third World, Group of Seven.

21. Awards and decorations are capitalized: Order of Canada, OC; Victoria Cross, VC. University degrees are lowercased except when abbreviated: master of arts, a master's, MA; doctor of philosophy, PhD.

22. Proper nouns and adjectives now regarded as common nouns are lowercased: brussels sprouts, french fries, draconian, scotch.

23. For all-capital corporate and promotional names, capitalize only the first letters: Via, Visa. For names consisting of two or more words written solid, follow the organization's capitalization: TVOntario, MuchMusic. Uppercase the first letter of corporate and promotional names even if the organization's style is lowercase: Adidas, EBay. For names of people or performing groups, follow their preference, as long as it doesn't excessively hamper readability.

For a fuller treatment of capitalization,
see the CP Stylebook, chapter Capitalization.

Spelling

1. The *Canadian Oxford Dictionary* is the authority for Canadian Press spelling with specific exceptions noted in the *CP Stylebook* and this guide. Where optional forms are given — moustache, mustache — the first listed is CP style.
2. When the spelling of the common-noun element of a proper name differs from CP style – Center Harbor, N.H., Lincoln Center, Canadian Paediatric Society – use the spelling favoured by the subject. One exception is names of government departments and agencies. Use U.S. Defence (not Defense) Department and U.S. Labour (not Labor) Department to avoid inconsistency with other words likely to be found in the story, such as defence secretary and labour legislation.
3. CP ignores symbols and unnecessary punctuation in corporate or other names or translates them into accepted punctuation if necessary: 'N Sync, not *NSYNC; the Bravo TV channel, not Bravo!; Mamma Mia, not Mamma Mia! Check individual listings.
4. CP style is -our, not -or, for labour, honour and other such words of more than one syllable in which the "u" is not pronounced:

arbour	ardour	armour
behaviour	candour	clamour
clangour	colour	demeanour
discolour	dishonour	enamour
endeavour	favour	fervour
flavour	glamour	harbour
honour	humour	labour
neighbour	odour	parlour
rancour	rigour	rumour
saviour	savour	splendour
tumour	valour	vapour
vigour		

Spelling

5. In some forms of these words, however, the "u" is dropped, especially when an -ous ending is added: laborious, rancorous, odorous, honorary.

6. For words in common use, CP style is simple "e" rather than the diphthongs "ae" and "oe." Thus CP style is archeologist, ecumenical, encyclopedia, esthetic, fetus, gynecologist, hemorrhage, medieval, paleontologist, pedagogy and pediatrician.

7. Generally, proper names retain the diphthong: Caesar, Oedipus, Phoebe. Also hors d'oeuvre, manoeuvre and subpoena. The "ae" in aerial, aerate and such is considered normal spelling.

8. The umlaut — ä, ö and ü — in German names is indicated by the letter "e" after the letter affected. Thus: Goering for Göring.

9. The -ov and -ev endings for Russian names are used instead of -off and -eff. Exceptions include such familiar names as Rachmaninoff, Smirnoff and Ignatieff, where the spelling is established.

10. CP style for First Nations names is to follow the preference of the band. For a current list of bands and their preferred spellings, check the Publications and Research page (community profiles) on the website of the Department of Indian and Northern Affairs (www.inac.gc.ca).

11. For Arabic names, use an English spelling that approximates the way a name sounds in Arabic. If an individual has a preferred spelling in English, use it.

12. Use the Ukrainian, not the Russian, transliteration for Ukrainian place names: Chornobyl (not Chernobyl); Kyiv (not Kiev).

Abbreviations

1. All-capital abbreviations are written without periods (YMCA, AFL-CIO, CN, MP, URL, RIP,) unless the abbreviation is geographical (U.S., B.C., P.E.I., T.O., U.K.) refers to a person (J.R. Ewing) or is a single letter (N. for north but NNW).
2. Most lowercase and mixed abbreviations take periods: f.o.b., Jr., Ont., No., B.Comm.
3. Mixed abbreviations that begin and end with a capital letter do not take periods: PhD, PoW, U of T.
4. Acronyms — abbreviations pronounced as words — formed from only the first letter of each principal word are all capitals: AIDS (acquired immune deficiency syndrome), NATO (North Atlantic Treaty Organization), NOW (National Organization for Women).
5. Acronyms formed from initial and other letters are upper and lowercase: Dofasco (Dominion Foundries and Steel Corp.), Nabisco (National Biscuit Co.), Norad (North American Aerospace Defence Command).
6. Acronyms that have become common words are not capitalized: laser (light amplification by stimulated emission of radiation), radar (radio detection and ranging).
7. Metric symbols are not abbreviations and do not take periods: m, l, kW.
8. Plurals are MPs and PoWs; possessives MPs' and PoWs'.
9. Most abbreviations are written without spaces: U.K., W.Va., P.Eng. But those written without periods are spaced: U of T.
10. Ampersands are allowed if used as part of a corporate name: A&W, Standard & Poor's, and in expressions like R&B. Usually, these are

Abbreviations

written without spaces when all-capital abbreviations are used and with spaces when they are not. Check individual listings.

See also the CP Stylebook, chapter Abbreviations and acronyms.

Place Names

1. National Geographic Society spellings are CP style for place names outside Canada with exceptions listed in the *CP Stylebook* and this guide.

2. The style authority for Canadian place names is the *Canadian Oxford Dictionary*, with some exceptions listed in this guide. If the place name is not in *Oxford*, consult the Secretariat of the Canadian Permanent Committee on Geographical Names (http://geonames.nrcan.gc.ca). For French place names, see next page.

French Capitalization

1. For the French names of organizations and the titles of books, songs, plays, movies, paintings and the like, CP prefers the English form for the sake of readability: Quebec Liquor Corp., not Société des alcools du Québec; Remembrance of Things Past, not A la recherche du temps perdu.

2. In general, when the French name or title is used (in a quotation, for example) it should be followed by a description in English or a translation: Office de la langue française, or the government language agency; Le Malade imaginaire (The Imaginary Invalid).

3. If a work, organization or the like is commonly known by its French name, it need not be followed by a translation: La Bohème, Notre Dame, Le Droit.

4. The names of some organizations cannot really be translated (Conseil du patronat, the largest employer group in Quebec), or have become familiar in their French version (the Ecole polytechnique, the engineering school), or have no official English version (the Centrale des syndicats du Québec, the union that represents teachers).

5. CP uses hyphens in multi-word French place names in Quebec and abroad: Trois-Rivières, Ste-Anne-de-Beaupré, Stanstead-Est, Ver-sur-Mer. Hyphens are omitted from purely English place names: Stanstead Plain, and if the first word is not a place name but a natural feature: Lac Barrière, Baie des Chaleurs.

6. For the names of saints (except in place names) use St. (not Ste.) for female as well as male: St. Dorothee.

7. CP's French dictionaries are *Le Petit Robert* and *Le Petit Larousse.*

French Names

1. For the names of organizations, the first word is capitalized unless it is an article; other words except proper nouns are lowercase: (le) Service de perception, Emballages St-Laurent ltée.
2. For the titles of books, songs and the like, the first word is capitalized — the second too when the first is an article — and proper nouns: De la terre à la lune, Sur le pont d'Avignon, Les Liaisons dangereuses.
3. For the names of newspapers, the definite article, the first noun and proper nouns are capitalized: Le Journal de Montréal, Le Courrier du peuple.

A, An–Use "a" before consonant sounds: a historic building, a university, a one-way ticket, a euphemism, a 1914 novel. Use "an" before vowel sounds: an apple, an honest man, an S-bend, an 1814 novel, an RRSP.

A&E (specialty TV channel)

A&P (acceptable in all references for Great Atlantic and Pacific Tea Co.), A&P Canada

A&W

ABC (acceptable in all references for American Broadcasting Cos. – note plural)

Abbott, Sir John (prime minister, 1891-92)

abhor, abhorrence, abhorrent

Abidjan

Abitibi-Consolidated Inc. (TSX:A)

able seaman (*no abbvn.*)

Ablonczy, Diane (politician)

A-bomb

abominable snowman (yeti)

aboriginal (*adj., n. when referring to individual*); in Australia: Aboriginal or Aborigine

Aboriginal Peoples (all of Canada's Indians, Inuit and Métis)

abscess

abysmal (*not* -ss-)

abyss

Acadie nouvelle, L' (newspaper in Caraquet, N.B.)

accessible (*not* -able)

accommodate (-mm-), accommodation

acetaminophen

acetylene

acetylsalicylic acid (ASA)

Achilles heel, tendon

acknowledgment

acquit, acquitted, acquittal

Act–Capitalize titles of parliamentary acts but not

subsequent references when the full name is not used. And references to acts and bills before royal assent are lowercase.
–Food and Drugs Act
–the food act says ...
–a proposed food act

Act 3, Scene 2; the third act, second scene

acting, acting mayor James Borden, acting Sgt. Jane Bloom

Action démocratique du Québec (ADQ or Action démocratique *on second reference*)

actor (OK for both men and women)

ACTRA (Alliance of Canadian Cinema, Television and Radio Artists)

AD–Acceptable in all references for anno Domini (in the year of the Lord). The abbreviation goes before the figure for the year: AD 410. It may also be used to refer to a century: the first century AD.

adaptability

addendum, addenda

Addresses–Capitalize Street, Road, etc., used with names; *but* King and Victoria streets.
Abbreviate in addresses when the number is used; *but* 10 Downing Street, 24 Sussex Drive (official residences).
–36 King St. E., Toronto M5C 2L9
–the Portage Avenue bus
–Wellington Crescent
–Cres., Blvd., Rd., Sq.

Adidas (*not* adidas)

adieu, adieus

adjuster (*not* -or)

administration, U.S. administration

Admiral John Smith (*no abbvn.*)
–the admiral said ...

admiralty
>−the admiralty reported ...
>−first lord of the admiralty
>−the first lord's statement
>−Admiralty Court

admissible (*not* -able), admissibility

ad nauseam (*not* -eum)

Adonai

adrenalin

Adventist, Seventh-day

adverse (unfavourable), averse (reluctant)

advertise (*not* -ize)

adviser (*not* -or)

aerial

aerodynamics

Aeroflot airline

Aeronautics Act

aesthetic – *Use* esthetic

AF and AM (for Ancient Free and Accepted
>Masons, *but avoid*)
>−a Freemason, a Mason

affect (*v.* – have effect on)

affidavit

affront (deliberate insult), effrontery (shameless
>insolence)

Afghan (*n.* and *adj.*, *prefer to* Afghani)

aficionado (*one f*), aficionados

AFL-CIO (acceptable in all references for American
>Federation of Labor-Congress of Industrial
>Organizations)

African-American

African Union (AU, *but avoid*)

Afrikaans (language)

Afrikaner (person)

Aga Khan, the

Agence France-Presse (AFP)

agenda, agendas
agent provocateur, agents provocateurs
aggression, aggressive
aging (*not* ageing)
Aglukark, Susan
agreement
–a Canada-U.S. agreement on power
–General Agreement on Tariffs and Trade
(GATT)
aide-de-camp, aides-de-camp
AIDS (for acquired immune deficiency syndrome)
airbag
airbase
Airbus
Air Canada (*no abbvn.*)
–ACE Aviation Holdings Inc. (parent
company; TSX:ACE.B)
Air Commodore John Smith (*no abbvn.*)
–the air commodore said ...
Aircraft Names – Use a hyphen between symbols
for the make or type and the model number.
–DC-8L, B-57, A-320, MiG-25, CF-18
–Yak-42, AN-154, IL-62, TU-144
–*but* Dash 8 (*no hyphen*)
aircrew (*one word*)
airdrop (*one word*)
Air Force–Capitalize air force in references to the
pre-unification Royal Canadian Air Force. For
other forces, lowercase air force when
preceded by the name of the country.
–British air force
–Royal Air Force
–U.S. or American air force
–U.S. 8th Air Force
–the air force planes
–Bomber Command

—Fleet Air Arm
—126 Squadron
—the squadron headquarters are ...
Air India (*no hyphen*)
airlift (*n.* and *v.*)
Air Line Pilots Association (ALPA)
airmail (*n.* and *v.*)
airman (*no abbvn.*)
Air Marshal Lois Jones (*no abbvn.*)
—the air marshal said ...
Air Miles (loyalty program)
Airport–Lowercase unless the official name is
used.
—Pearson International Airport
—Toronto international airport
—Vancouver International Airport
—the Vancouver airport
air strike
Air Vice-Marshal John Candy (*no abbvn.*)
—the air vice-marshal
a.k.a.
Aklavik, N.W.T.
Akwesasne Mohawk Territory
Al–In Arabic names of individuals, the articles el
and al may be used or dropped depending
on the person's preference or established
usage: Ayman al-Zawahri, al-Zawahri (*second
reference*); *but* Moammar Gadhafi, Gadhafi.
For other names, the article is usually
uppercase: Al-Jazeera (Arab all-news satellite
channel)
Alabama (Ala.)
Alaska (*no abbvn.*)
Alberta (Alta.)
Alberta Heritage Savings Trust Fund (*no abbvn.*)
Alcan Inc. (TSX:AL)

Alcoholics Anonymous (AA)
    –Al-Anon (for relatives of alcoholics)
    –Alateen (for children of alcoholics)
alderman, alderwoman (Ald.)
    –Ald. John Doe
    –alderwomen Jill Jones and Julia Wong
Alderwoods Group Inc. – formerly Loewen Group
    Inc.
Algonquian (aboriginal language family)
Algonquin (Ojibwa dialect)
Allah
Allahu akbar! (God is great)
all-America (team), all-American (individual)
Allan Cup (hockey)
Alliance Atlantis Communications Inc.
    (TSX:AAC.NV.B)
Alliance of Canadian Cinema, Television and Radio
    Artists (ACTRA)
Allied forces, the Allies (in world wars)
allophone (*but avoid*)
allot, allotted, allotting
all ready (set to go), already (beforehand)
all right (*two words; not* alright)
All Saints' Day (Nov. 1)
all-star
    –an all-star team, game
    –CP's all-star selections
    –National League All-Stars (team)
allusion (indirect reference), illusion (false
    impression)
Almighty, the
Alouette 1, 2 (satellites)
Alps, *but* alpine skiing
al-Qaida
already (beforehand)
alternate (one after the other), alternative (one or

the other)

aluminum

alumna, alumnae (*fem.*)

alumnus, alumni

Alzheimer's disease (*but* Alzheimer Society of
Canada)

a.m., p.m. (*lowercase*)
   —2 p.m., 2:30 a.m. EST, EDT

a mari usque ad mare (from sea to sea)

ambassador, the U.S. ambassador
   —Ambassador Frank McKenna (capitalize
   before a name)

Amber Alert (child-abduction response system)

ambience

Ambrozic, Aloysius (Roman Catholic cardinal and
   Archbishop of Toronto)

amendment, Fifth Amendment (U.S.)

American Federation of Labor-Congress of
   Industrial Organizations (AFL-CIO)

American Indian Movement (AIM)

American Telephone and Telegraph Co. (AT&T)

America's Cup (yachting)

amiable (of people), amicable (of things)

amok (*not* amuck)

Ampersand – Use when part of a corporate name:
   H&R Block and in expressions such as B&B
   (bed and breakfast). Write out in other uses:
   Ian and Sylvia.

Amtrak (*not* Amtrack)

analogous

analysis, analyses

analyze (*not* -se), analyzing

anemia, anemic

anesthesia, anesthetic, anesthetist

aneurysm

Anglican Church of Canada

–Anglican communion
–Anglican Church Women
–High Church, Low Church
Anglo, Anglo-Quebecer, Anglos
anglophone (*lowercase*)
Anik F-1, F-2 (satellites)
Animals–Capitalize breed names derived from
proper names except where usage has
established the lowercase.
–Holstein-Friesian *but* shorthorn
–Clydesdale *but* palomino
–Newfoundland dog *but* dachshund
–Siamese cat *but* angora
anoint
anomaly, anomalies
anorexia nervosa, anorexic
ante (prefix), antechamber, antedate, antenatal,
anteroom
antenna, antennae (*pl.* for feelers of insect, etc.),
antennas (*pl.* for aerials)
anti- (*prefix*), anti-aircraft, anti-Communist,
antihistamine, anti-intellectual, anti-Semitic,
antitrust, antivirus, antiwar
antivenin (*not* anti-venom)
anybody
anyhow
anymore (any longer)
any more (*as in* "I don't want any more candy")
anyone
anyplace
anything
any time (*two words*)
anyway
AOL Time Warner
–AOL Canada Inc.
apartheid

Apartment–Capitalize when used specifically, as when followed by a number; abbreviate when used in numbered addresses.
–the Rockingham Apartments
–in Apt. 207
–Apt. 207, Midtown Terrace
APEC (Asia-Pacific Economic Cooperation)
apostle, Twelve Apostles
–the Apostle Paul
–Paul the Apostle
appal, appalled, appalling
Appaloosa
apparatus, apparatuses
appeal, appealed, appealing, appealingly
Appeal Court
appellant
appellate division (of Supreme Court)
appendix, appendixes
Apples–Capitalize varieties.
–McIntosh, Golden Delicious, Ida Red
April (*no abbvn.*)
April Fool's Day (April 1)
Aqaba, Gulf of
Aqua-Lung (trademark for an underwater breathing device)
aquarium, aquariums
arabic numerals
Arafat, Yasser (PLO)
Aransas (*not* Arkansas) refuge
arbour
arc, arcing, arced
Arcand, Denys (movies)
Archbishop–Capitalize before a name and when the full title is used.
–Archbishop John Smith
–Archbishop of York

–the archbishop said ...

archdiocese, Toronto archdiocese

archeological, archeologist, archeology

Arctic–Capitalize when referring to the Arctic
region: Arctic Circle, Arctic Ocean, Arctic char,
Arctic fox, Arctic plant. Lowercase when it
meaning very cold: arctic chill, arctic
temperatures.

Arden, Jann (musician)

ardour

Argentine (*not* Argentinian)

argyle socks, sweater

Argyll and Sutherland Highlanders of Canada

Arizona (Ariz.)

Arkansas (Ark.) *but* Aransas refuge (for wildlife)

Armed Forces, the Forces (capped for Canada only)

armful, armfuls

armour

arm's-length *(adj.)*

Army–Capitalize Canadian Army when referring to
pre-unification force. For other forces,
lowercase army when preceded by the name
of the country.
–Canadian Army until 1968
–British army
–British 21st Army
–a convoy of army vehicles
–1st Canadian Division
–3rd Infantry Brigade
–Royal 22nd Regiment
–1st Battalion, Royal 22nd
–B Company

Art–Lowercase art styles, schools, movements, etc.,
unless the word is derived from a proper
noun or can be confused with a common
word.

—art deco, art nouveau
 —baroque
 —cubism, cubist
 —Dada, Dadaism
 —Gothic
 —impressionism, impressionist
 —neoclassical
 —Renaissance
 —Romanesque
arteriosclerosis
Arthabaska, Que. (Athabasca, Alta.)
arthroscopy
article
 —a paragraph of Article 4
 —Art. 4, Sec. 1, reads:
artifact
Arviat, Nunavut (formerly Eskimo Point)
Aryan Nations (white supremacist group)
ascend, ascendance, ascendant, ascension, ascent
 —Ascension Day
Ashrawi, Hanan (Palestinian)
Ash Wednesday
asinine
Aspirin (trademark in Canada)
Assad, Hafez (Syria)
assassin, assassination
assembly
 —National Assembly (national legislative
 body)
 —Quebec national assembly (provincial body)
 —legislative assembly
assistant (*lowercase*), assistant attorney general
 Erin Keenan
assizes, spring assizes
Associated Press, The (for AP)
 —and The Associated Press said ...

–the Associated Press story said ...

–the AP (*second reference; lowercase* the)

Association of South East Asian Nations (ASEAN)

Associations–Capitalize names, but follow French style for French names.

–Société pour vaincre la pollution

–Association of the Scientific, Engineering and Technological Community of Canada (Scitec)

–Canadian Bankers Association

–the association meeting

Astronomy–Capitalize the proper names of planets, stars, constellations; capitalize only the proper-noun element of the name of comets, etc.; lowercase sun and moon. In general, lowercase earth, but capitalize it when referred to as an astronomical body.

–Saturn, North Star, Orion

–Halley's comet, Crab nebula

–down to earth

–heaven on earth

–The planets closest to the sun are Mercury, Venus and Earth.

–The astronauts turned back to Earth.

Astroturf (trademark for artificial grass or turf)

AT&T (*no spaces*), for American Telephone and Telegraph Co.

Athabasca, Alta. (Arthabaska, Que.)

Athapaskan (aboriginal languages)

atherosclerosis (a form of arteriosclerosis with fatty degeneration)

Athlete of the Year

Athletes Can (*not* CAN)

athlete's foot

Atikamekw (First Nations in Quebec)

Atlantic provinces (N.B., N.L., N.S., P.E.I.)

Atomic Energy of Canada Ltd. (AECL, *but avoid*)
attorney, Crown
     –Crown attorney Ellen Tomcik
     –power of attorney (*no hyphens*)
attorney general, attorneys general
     –Attorney General Madalene Phillips
Audit Bureau of Circulations (ABC)
auditor general, auditors general
auger (tool for boring holes)
augur (bode)
Augustyn, Frank (ballet)
aurora borealis (northern lights); aurora
     australis (southern equivalent)
     –Aurora (patrol aircraft)
authority
     –St. Lawrence Seaway Authority
authorize
automaker, autoworker (*but* Canadian Auto
     Workers union)
automaton, automatons
auto pact (signed January 1965)
Avenue–Capitalize when used with names;
     abbreviate in numbered street addresses.
     –along Portage Avenue
     –the Portage Avenue bus
     –506 Curry Ave., Windsor, Ont. N9B 2B9
averse (reluctant), adverse (unfavourable)
avocado, avocados
Avro Arrow (the CF-105 interceptor aircraft built
     by A.V. Roe Canada Ltd. in the 1950s)
AWACS (for airborne warning and control system)
Awards–Capitalize specific awards.
     –National Newspaper Awards (NNA)
     –the awards were presented ...
     –Governor General's Awards
     –Governor General's Award for poetry

    –Nobel Peace Prize
    –Nobel Prize in chemistry
    –Nobel Prize winner
    –Pulitzer Prize
    –Pulitzer Prize-winning author
    –Academy Awards

awhile *(adv.), but* a while *(n.)*

AWL (*not* AWOL – absent without leave; *but avoid*)

axe (*not* ax), axing

Axel (figure-skating jump)

axis, axes
    –Axis, the (Second World War alliance of Germany, Italy and Japan)

Aykroyd, Dan (comic)

Azerbaijan

AZT (HIV-AIDS drug, often called zidovudine)

B

Baathist party (Iraq)
baby boom, baby boomer, baby boom generation
babysit, babysitter
baccalaureate
Bachand, Claude (politician)
bachelor
    –bachelor of arts (BA), a bachelor's degree
    –bachelor of laws (LLB, *but avoid)*
    –bachelor of science (B.Sc.)
bacillus, bacilli
backbench members, backbenchers, backbenches
backbone, backlog, backstop (*n.* and *v.*), backyard
back burner, back roads
backstage
backup *(n.* and *adj.)*
bacterium, bacteria
Baha'i (*n.* and *adj.*)
    –two Baha'is
    –the Baha'i faith
Bahamas, the
Bahamian (*not* Bahaman)
Bahrain
bail (water or bond)
bail out (of plane)
baked alaska
balaclava
bale (hay)
balk
balkanize
ball, ball club, ball game *but* ballplayer, ballpark
balloon, ballooning, balloonist
ballot, balloting
ballpoint
ballroom, Crystal Ballroom
baloney (slang – nonsense; also informal –
    bologna sausage)

band, the God's River band
Band-Aid (trademark for an adhesive bandage)
B&B (*no spaces*), bed and breakfast
banister (*not* -nn-)
banjo, banjos
Banks–Short forms may be used on first reference
  when their use is widespread.
  –Bank of Canada
  –the bank's lending policy
  –Bank of Nova Scotia, Scotiabank
  –Canadian Imperial Bank of Commerce,
CIBC
  –HSBC Bank Canada
  –Royal Bank of Canada, the Royal Bank
  –TD Bank Financial Group, Toronto-
Dominion Bank
  –World Bank
baptize (*not* -s-)
bar
  –Canadian Bar Association (CBA, *but avoid*)
  –Bar of the Province of Quebec (organization)
  –*but* Quebec bar, Montreal bar, called to the
bar
Barbados (one island; *do not use* the Barbados)
barbecue (*not* -que), barbecuing
barbiturate
Bardot, Brigitte
barefoot (*no hyphen*)
bar mitzvah (for boy marking 13th birthday), bat
  mitzvah (for girl)
Barnard, Dr. Christiaan (1922-2001)
baroque
Barren Lands, the Barrens
Barrick Gold Inc. (TSX:HCX)
Barron's (financial weekly published by Dow
  Jones)

B

Baryshnikov, Mikhail (ballet)

Baseball–at bat (*but* five at-bats), backstop, ball club, ballpark, ballplayer, baseline, bullpen, centre field, centre-fielder, centre-field fence, change-up, double-A, doubleheader, double-play, earned-run average, fastball, first baseman, home plate, home run, left-fielder, left-hander, line up (*v.*), lineup (*n.*), major league (*n.*), major-league (*adj.*), a major-leaguer (*n.*), pinch hit (*n.* and *v.*), pinch-hitter (*n.*), play off (*v.*), playoff (*n., adj.*), RBI(s), put out (*v.*), putout (*n.*), right-fielder, right-hander, shortstop, shut out (*v.*), shutout (*n., adj.*), single-A, split-finger fastball, triple-A, triple-play, twi-night doubleheader

Basel, Switzerland

BASIC (for beginner's all-purpose symbolic instruction code)

basis, bases

Basketball–backboard, backcourt, baseline, field goal, foul line, foul shot, free throw, free-throw line, frontcourt, full-court press, goaltending, half-court pass, halftime, in-bounds pass, jump ball, jump shot, layup, man-to-man (*adj.*), midcourt, play off (*v.*), playoff (*n., adj.*), three-point play, three-pointer

basset (dog)

battalion, 3rd Battalion

Battle Harbour, N.L.

Battles–Capitalize specific ones.
   –Battle of the Plains of Abraham
   –Battle of Britain

bay, Hudson Bay, Bay of Quinte
   –Hudson's Bay Co., the Bay

bazaar

B

BB (shot)

BC–Acceptable in all references for before Christ. It
  follows the year or the century: 55 BC, the
  second century BC.

BCE Inc. (TSX:BCE)
  –Bell Canada
  –Bell ExpressVu
  –Bell Globemedia
  –Bell Mobility
  –Sympatico (Internet portal)

beau, beaus

beef Stroganoff

Beethoven, Ludwig van (*not* von) (1770-1827)

behaviour

behoove (*not* behove)

Beijing (formerly Peking)

Belarus (formerly Byelorussia), Belarusian

Belize (formerly British Honduras)

Bell Canadian Open (men's golf tournament)

belligerent

bellwether

Belmont Stakes

beluga (whale)

benefit, benefited, benefiting

Benin (Dahomey until 1975)

Bergeron, Stéphane (politician)

Berkeley, Calif.

Berlin Wall

Bermudian (*not* Bermudan)

Bern, Switzerland

Bernhard, Prince (Netherlands)

berserk

Berton, Pierre (1920-2004)

besieged (*not* beseiged)

bestseller (*one word*), bestselling author

bettor (one who wagers)

Beverly Hills, Calif.

Bevilacqua, Maurizio (politician)

BHP Billiton Ltd. (Australia-based mining
company)

Bible, Bible Belt

–*but* the fisherman's bible

biblical

Bic (trademark for pen)

bicultural, bilingual (*no hyphen*)

Biennial, bimonthly, biweekly–These terms are
ambiguous and can mean two different
things. *Prefer* every two years, twice a
month, twice a week, etc.

Big Three, Big Ten

big-time (*adj.*), big time (*n.*)

bill

–Bill 101

–a proposed bill of rights

billet, billeted, billeting

Binghamton, N.Y.

bin Laden, Osama

bioterrorism, bioterrorist

biracial (*no hyphen*)

birdie (one stroke under par in golf)

Birks Jewellers (store)

–Henry Birks and Sons Inc.

Birney, Earle (poet, 1904-1995)

birth, birthday, birthmark, birthrate, birthright

Bishkek, Kyrgyzstan (formerly Frunze, Kirghizia)

Bishop–Capitalize before a name and when the full
title is used.

–Bishop Edward Tremaine

–Bishop of London

–the bishop's letter

Bismarck (*not* -rk)

black (*prefer to* Negro)

BlackBerry (wireless device)
blackfly, blackflies
Blackhawks, Chicago
Black Muslim (member of Black Muslims
  organization; official name: the Nation of
  Islam)
black out (*v.*), blackout (*n.* and *adj.*)
Black Panther (member of Black Panthers
  organization)
Blaikie, Bill (politician)
bleached-kraft pulp
blindsided
bloc (of parties, countries; voted as a bloc)
  –Bloc Québécois
  –former East Bloc
block (of shares, seats; also mental block)
blond (*n.* and *adj.* for all uses; do not use blonde)
Blondin-Andrew, Ethel (politician)
bloodbath *(one word)*
Bloody Mary (nickname for Mary I), bloody mary
  (cocktail)
blue, Double Blue (Argonauts)
blue-line (hockey)
Bluenose II (ship)
BMO Financial Group Canadian Women's Open
  (golf tournament)
B'nai Brith (Sons of the Covenant)
Board–Uppercase when using the formal name of a
  board. Otherwise, lowercase.
  –Toronto District School Board, but Toronto
  school board, public school board
  –Board of Trade, the board
  –Canadian Wheat Board, the wheat board
  –Treasury Board, the board
boat, lifeboat, motorboat, powerboat, sailboat
bobsled, bobsledding

–Bobsleigh Canada

bocce (game)

bodycheck

bodyguard (*no hyphen*)

boe per day (*prefer* barrels of oil equivalent per day*)*

bogey, bogeys, bogeyed (for one over par)

bohemian (unconventional); Bohemian (of Czech region)

boldface (type)

Bomarc-A, Bomarc-B

bombardier (*no abbvn.*)

Bombardier Inc. (TSX:BBD.SV.B)

Bombay – *Use* Mumbai

bombshell (*one word*)

bona fide (*adj.* – genuine; *adv.* – genuinely), bona fides (*n.* – proof of status)

bonspiel

bonus, bonuses

bookkeeper, bookkeeping

Book of Common Prayer

Book of Revelation (*not* Revelations)

Bophuthatswana (former homeland state in South Africa)

borscht, Borscht Belt

Bosnia-Herzegovina, Bosnia

Bouctouche, N.B.

Boulevard–Capitalize when used with names; abbreviate in numbered street addresses.
–on Decarie Boulevard
–123 Decarie Blvd.

bound (*suffix*), eastbound, northbound, stormbound

bourbon (whisky)

Bourgeoys, St. Marguerite (Canada's first woman saint, 1620-1700)

Boutros-Ghali, Boutros (UN)

bovine spongiform encephalopathy (better known
        as mad cow disease; BSE OK *but explain*)
bowl, Rose Bowl, Super Bowl
bowling
        –fivepin, tenpin
boxcar
boyfriend, girlfriend
Boxing–Most weight classes are one word:
        flyweight, bantamweight, heavyweight.
        –knockout
boy scout – *See scout*
braggadocio
braille
Brantford Expositor
Brascan Corp. (TSX:BNN.A)
Brasilia (capital of Brazil)
Bravo (*not* Bravo!) specialty TV channel
breach (*n.* – breaking or neglect; *v.*   break
        through)
break (*n.*), breakaway, breakdown, break-in,
        breakneck, breakout, breakup, breakthrough,
        breakwater
break (*v.*), break away, break down, break even,
        break in, break off, break out, break up
breastfeed
breathalyser
Brébeuf, St. Jean de (1593-1649)
breech (back part of gun barrel), breeches (short
        trousers), breeches-buoy
Breitkreuz, Garry (politician)
Bren gun
Bre-X Minerals Ltd. (defunct)
Brezhnev, Leonid (1906-1982)
bridge, Lions Gate Bridge, Sydney Harbour Bridge
Brier (curling tournament), Tim Hortons Brier
brigadier (Brig. Arthur Smith)

B

brigadier-general (Brig.-Gen. Arthur Smith)

Brink's Canada Ltd.
>   –*but* a Brinks truck, Brinks guard (*no apostrophe*)

Britain–The one island: England, Scotland, Wales. (*But* British also covers Northern Ireland.)

Britannia

British Airways (*no abbvn.*)

British Columbia (B.C.)

British Commonwealth (*prefer* the Commonwealth)

British North America Act (BNA Act)

British thermal unit(s), BTU(s)

Briton (*not* Britisher)

broach (open; begin to talk about)

broccoli

Brockville Recorder and Times

Bromo Seltzer (trademark for bicarbonate of soda)

brooch (ornament)

Bros. for company names *but* Brothers with entertainment groups: the Mills Brothers

brouhaha

brussels sprouts

Brzezinski, Zbigniew

Buckingham Palace

Buddha, Buddhism, Buddhist

budget, budgetary, budgeted, budgeting

buffalo, buffaloes

Building–Capitalize important buildings.
>   –Parliament Buildings
>   –Empire State Building
>   –Aetna Life building

build up (*v.*), buildup (*n., adj.*), built-up (*adj*)

Bujold, Geneviève (actor)

bulimia

bullmastiff (*one word*)

Bullock, Sandra (actor)

bull's-eye
bumf (papers, documents)
bungee jumping
Bunyan, Paul
buoy, buoyant, buoyancy
bureau, bureaus
burka
Burkina Faso (formerly Upper Volta)
Burk's Falls, Ont.
Burton, Richard (actor, 1925-1984)
bus (vehicle), buses, busing
Busan, South Korea (*not* Pusan)
Bush, George W. (use initial to distinguish from
    father, George Bush)
businessman, businesswoman
buss (kiss), busses
Buthelezi, Mangosuthu (Zulu leader)
buttonhole (*no hyphen*)
byelection (*no hyphen*)
bylaw (*no hyphen*)
byline (*no hyphen*)
bypass (*no hyphen*)
byproduct (*no hyphen*)
byte (unit of computer memory)

C

cabinet, cabinet council
cable TV (*no hyphen*)
cacophony
cactus, cacti
cadet
     –officer cadet (*no abbvn.*)
     –Officer Cadet Garth Atkins
Cadillac
CAE Inc. (TSX:CAE)
Caesar, Julius (c. 102-44 BC)
caesarean birth, section (*lowercase*), *but* C-section
caesar salad
Caesars Palace (Las Vegas – *no apostrophe*)
café
caffeine
Cage, Nicolas (actor)
caisse populaire (credit union), caisses populaires
Calder Memorial Trophy (NHL's top rookie)
calibre, a .45-calibre pistol
California (Calif.)
Callaghan, Morley (novelist, 1903-1990)
Callbeck, Catherine (senator)
callisthenics
Call-Net Enterprises Inc. (TSX:FON.NV.B)
callous (*adj.* – unfeeling), callus (*n.* – thickened skin)
call-up (*n.*)
calorie
camaraderie
Cambodia (Kampuchea 1975-90)
Canada
     –Central Canada (Ontario and Quebec)
     –Eastern Canada (the Atlantic provinces,
     Quebec and Ontario)
     –Lower Canada (present-day Quebec)
     –Upper Canada (present-day Ontario)
     –Western Canada (Manitoba, Saskatchewan,

C

Alberta and British Columbia)
Canada AM (CTV show)
Canada Council for the Arts, Canada Council, the
     council
Canada Cup (hockey)
Canada Customs, customs
     —go through customs, a customs officer
Canada Day (July 1)
Canada Industrial Relations Board (CIRB, *but avoid*)
Canada Mortgage and Housing Corp. (CMHC)
Canada NewsWire (CNW in second reference)
Canadarm 2
Canada Pension Plan (CPP, *but avoid*)
Canada Revenue Agency (formerly Canada
     Customs and Revenue Agency)
Canada Savings Bond (CSB)
Canada's Cup (yachting)
Canada West Foundation
Canada-wide (*adj.*)
Canadian Alliance (now Conservative Party of
     Canada)
Canadian Association of Broadcasters (CAB)
Canadian Auto Workers (CAW *in second reference*)
Canadian Bankers Association
Canadian Blood Services
Canadian Coast Guard
     —the coast guard ship
     —coastguardman (*one word*)
Canadian Community Newspapers Association
Canadian Conference of Catholic Bishops (*not* Council)
Canadian Food Inspection Agency
Canadian Forces, the Forces (*capped for Canadian only*)
     —Canadian Forces Headquarters (CFHQ, *but avoid*)
     —a Canadian Forces base
     —Canadian Forces Base Trenton, CFB Trenton
     (*second reference*)

–CFB TRENTON (placeline)

Canadian government

Canadian Heritage (for Department of Canadian Heritage; *do not use* Heritage Canada, which is an unrelated organization)

Canadian Hockey Association – *See Hockey Canada*

Canadian Imperial Bank of Commerce–*See* CIBC

Canadian Institutes of Health Research (formerly Medical Research Council of Canada)

Canadian Interuniversity Sport (CIS *in second reference*)

Canadian Journalism Fellowships (formerly Southam Fellowships)
    –Canadian Journalism Fellow

Canadian Manufacturers & Exporters (formerly Alliance of Manufacturers & Exporters Canada)

Canadian National, or CN
    –Canadian National Railway Co. (formal name; TSX:CNR)
    –CN Tower

Canadian National Institute for the Blind (CNIB)

Canadian Newspaper Association (CNA, *but avoid)*

Canadian Nuclear Safety Commission (formerly Atomic Energy Control Board)

Canadian Opera Company (*not* Co.)

Canadian Pacific Railway Ltd. (TSX:CPR, formerly CP Rail)
    –CPR on second reference

Canadian Paediatric Society

Canadian Press, The (CP)
    –The Canadian Press says ...
    –*but* the Canadian Press reporter
    –CP services: Broadcast News, Command News, CPimages, CP Picture Archive, CP GraphicsNet, PR Direct

Canadian Professional Golfers' Association (CPGA)

C

Canadian Radio-television and
    Telecommunications Commission (CRTC *OK
    in first reference*)
Canadian Security Intelligence Service (CSIS)
Canadian Shield
Canadian Space Agency
Canadian Taxpayers Federation
Canadian Tire Corp. Ltd. (TSX:CTR.NV)
Canadian Transportation Agency
Canadian Wheat Board (*no abbvn.*)
Canadian Wildlife Service (*no abbvn.*)
canal, Panama Canal, Suez Canal, Welland Canal
    –Panama Canal Zone (district)
cancel, cancelled, cancelling
Cancer, Tropic of
CanCom, Canadian Satellite Communications Inc.
Cancon (*OK in second reference* for Canadian
    content)
candour
Candu (for Canadian deuterium uranium reactor)
Canfor Corp. (TSX:CFP)
canister
CanJet Airlines
canoeist
cantaloupe
canto, cantos
Canuck
canvas, canvases (cloth, painting)
canvass (*v.* – examine; seek votes, orders; *n.* –
    process of canvassing)
CanWest Global Communications Corp.
    (TSX:CGS.NV)
canyon, Grand Canyon
Cap-aux-Meules, Que.
Cape Breton (*never in placeline*)
Cape Town (*two words*)

C

Capitol (building at Washington, D.C.) *but* state
    capitol (*lowercase*)
cappuccino, cappuccinos
captain, Capt. (*but* team captain Joan Verona)
Cara Operations Ltd. (TSX:CAO.A)
carat (gems), karat (gold), caret (printing)
carburetor
cardinal (*no abbvn.*)
    –John Cardinal Smith
    –the cardinal (or Smith) said ...
CARE (for Co-operative for American Relief
    Everywhere Inc.)
caregiver
cargo, cargoes
Caribbean Community (federation)
Caribbean Free Trade Area (Carifta, *but avoid*)
Cariboo Mountains (B.C.)
Caribou Mountains (Alta.)
caribou (deer), Caribou (Inuit, plane)
carillon, carillonneur
carjack, carjacking (*v.* and *n.*)
Carleton, N.S. and Que.
    –Carleton Place, Ont.
    –Carleton University (Ottawa)
    –Carleton Village, N.S.
    –*but* Carlton, Sask.
    –Carlton Street (Toronto)
    –Ritz-Carlton Hotel
carmaker
carpet, carpet-bag, carpet-sweeper
Cartier, George-Etienne (1814-1873)
cartilage
cassette, videocassette
catalogue (*not* catalog)
catch-22 (a dilemma from which there is no
    escape); Catch-22 (Joseph Heller's book)

category, Category 2

Caterpillar, a Cat (trademark for a tractor)

catholic (universal)

Catholic, Catholicism (*but* specify Roman Catholic or Roman Catholicism *on first reference* if reference excludes Eastern-rites Catholic churches.

CAT scan – *Use* CT scan

Cattle–Capitalize breed names derived from proper names except where usage has established the lowercase.
 –Holstein-Friesian
 –Jersey, Guernsey, Ayrshire
 –shorthorn

Caucasian

cave in (*v.*), cave-in (*n.*)

CBC (*acceptable in all references* for Canadian Broadcasting Corp.)
 CBC-TV, CBC Radio One, CBC Radio Two
 –The Current, The National, Newsworld

CBS Inc. (formerly Columbia Broadcasting System, CBS *acceptable in all references*)
 –CBS's coverage

Cdn ($1,200 Cdn)

CD-ROM (compact disc read-only memory); *acceptable in all references*

cease fire (*v.*), ceasefire (*n.*)

Ceausescu, Nicolae (Romanian leader, 1918-1989)

Celanese (trademark for acetate, nylon, polyester, rayon)

Celestica Inc. (TSX:CLS)

cellblock (in jail)

cellophane, celluloid, cellulose

cellphone (cellular phone)

Celsius, -30 C (hyphen, no period;

specify Celsius only to avoid confusion)
cement (powder; used in concrete)
cemetery, Ocean View Cemetery
census, censuses
Centennial Year, the Centennial (1967)
> –*bu*t Canada's centennial
> –centennial celebrations

Centers for Disease Control and Prevention (Atlanta)
centimetre (cm – *sing.* and *pl.* metric symbol, no period)
Central Canada (Ontario and Quebec)
Central Committee
Centrale de l'enseignement du Québec (Quebec teachers federation)
centre, centred, centring
> –centre on (*not* around)
> –centre field (baseball)
> –centre-fielder
> –centre-field wall
> –John F. Kennedy Center for the Performing Arts
> –Air Canada Centre
> –Rockefeller Center

Centre of Forensic Sciences (Toronto)
centurion (Roman soldier), Centurion (tank)
century, 20th century, second-century Rome
CEO (*OK in first reference* for chief executive officer)
CFCs (chlorofluorocarbons)
CF-18 (Canadian designation for the McDonnell Douglas aircraft)
chamber, lower chamber
> –Chamber of Deputies
> –Halifax Chamber of Commerce
> –the chamber of commerce

changeover (*n*.), change over (*v*.)
channel
     –Channel 10 (television)
     –English Channel and the Channel
     –Channel Tunnel (between Britain and
     France)
chaperon (*not* -one)
Chappaquiddick Island, Mass.
chapter (*no abbvn.*), Chapter 1
chargeback (*n.* and *adj.*)
chargé(s) d'affaires, chargé d'affaires John O'Hara
charley horse
Charlottetown accord
Charter of Rights and Freedoms, the charter,
     charter rights
chat room
check (restaurant bill)
check off (*v.*), checkoff (*n*)
check up (*v.*), checkup (*n.*)
checkerboard, checkers, checkered flag (motor
     racing), checkered career
checkpoint (*one word*), Checkpoint Charlie
Chedabucto Bay, N.S.
cheddar cheese
chef-d'oeuvre, chefs-d'oeuvre
Chekhov, Anton (Russian writer, 1860-1904)
cheque (bank), chequebook
Chernomyrdin, Viktor (Russian politician)
cherub, cherubs
Chiang Kai-shek (1887-1975)
Chianti (wine)
chickenpox
chief
     –Chief Tom Whitefeather
     –police Chief Anna Myers
     –fire Chief Ron Espy

C

chief master sergeant
–Chief Master Sgt. Phil McDonald
chief petty officer (*no abbvn.*)
chief warrant officer (*no abbvn.*)
childish (silly, puerile), childlike (innocent,
trusting)
Children's Aid Society
Chile
chili, chilies
–chili con carne
–chili sauce
china (crockery)
China, People's Republic of (mainland, *but prefer
simply* China)
Chinese (*n* and *adj.*)
Chinese Names–Use the official Chinese spelling,
Pinyin, for most personal and place names:
Hua Guofeng (formerly Hua Kuofeng). Note
that the family name (Hua) normally
precedes the given name (Guofeng). But
westernized Chinese often follow English
practice: Robert Chow (*not* Chow Robert).
Use the traditional spellings for Shanghai and
Tibet. But use Zhou Enlai (*not* Chou En lai)
and Mao Zedong (*not* Mao Tse-tung).
chinook
Chipewyan (aboriginal band)
chipmaker (*one word*)
chisel, chiselled, chiseller
chlorophyll
choose, chose, chosen, choosing, choosy
Chornobyl (Ukraine)
Chou En-lai – *See Zhou Enlai*
Chrétien, Jean
Christie's (auctioneer)
Christmas Day, Eve

chromosome

CHUM Ltd. (TSX:CHM)

Church–Capitalize in names of religions and
buildings.

–Roman Catholic Church, Catholic Church,
Anglican Church; *but* the church (*lowercase*)

–St. Bartholomew's Church (building), the
church (building)

–a church building, church doctrine

Church of Christ, Scientist (Christian Science
Church *OK in first reference*)

Church of Jesus Christ of Latter-day Saints
(Mormons)

chute (sluice, slide, parachute)

chutzpah (gall, audacity)

CIBC (TSX:CM)

–CIBC (for Canadian Imperial Bank of
Commerce) *OK in first reference*

–CIBC World Markets Inc. (corporate and
investment banking arm); CIBC Wood
Gundy (retail investment division)

cigarette

cipher (*not* cypher)

circle (Circ.)

Circle, Arctic

–*but* arctic winds, temperatures

Cirque du soleil

cirrhosis

citizens band (CB, *but avoid*)

–citizens-band radio (*hyphen*)

city, city council

–Halifax City Hall (proper name)

–city hall (administration, building)

–City of Halifax (corp.)

–*but* in the city of Halifax

–Quebec City (Quebec in placelines)

Citytv (Toronto)

C

–CityPulse
–CablePulse 24
Civil Aeronautics Board (U.S.)
Civil Service Commission (*no abbvn.*)
civil war
–Spanish Civil War
–Civil War (U.S.)
clamour
clangour (*but* clangorous)
Claridge's (London hotel)
Clark, Joe (former prime minister)
Clarke, Austin (novelist)
Clarkson, Adrienne
Class–Lowercase school classes, except languages.
–class of '61
–mathematics class
–French class
class (military)
–S-class submarine
–tribal-class destroyer
clean up (*v.*), cleanup (*n.*)
clear cut (*v.*), clearcut (*n.*)
cliché
clientele
climactic (of a climax), climatic (of climate)
cloverleaf (on highways), cloverleafs
Club–Capitalize names.
–Rotary Club
–a club officer
CN–*See Canadian National*
CN Tower (Toronto)
co- (prefix), coadjutor, co-author (*n. only*), coaxial,
co-chairman, coed, coexist, co-host,
co-operate, co-ordinate, co-owner, co-pilot (*n.
only*), co-worker.
coast

–East Coast, West Coast, Gulf Coast (regions),
B.C. coast, Atlantic coast (shorelines)
coast guard
–Canadian Coast Guard
–U.S. Coast Guard
–the coast guard, the coast guard ship
cobalt-60
Cobol (common business oriented language)
Cobourg, Ont.
Coca-Cola, Coke (trademarks for cola drink)
coccus, cocci
cockney
Codco (comedy TV)
code, city building code
–Criminal Code, the code
–Morse code
Cogeco Cable Inc. (TSX:CCA.SV)
cognoscente (*sing.*), cognoscenti (*pl.*)
coho (salmon – *sing.* and *pl.*)
Coke (as trade name for Coca-Cola)
Cold War
Colisée (Quebec City arena)
collectible(s)
College–Capitalize the names of universities and
colleges.
–McGill University
–University of Toronto (U of T)
–Victoria College
College Degrees – *See University Degrees*
College of Cardinals
collegiate, York Collegiate (capitalize when part of
official name)
Collins Bay, Ont.
–Collins Bay Penitentiary
Colombia (South America)
Colombo Plan

C

colonel (Col. Eric Anderson)
Colorado (Colo.)
Colosseum (Rome)
colour, colourize, colourist *but* colorific
Colville, Alex (painter)
Comaneci, Nadia (former gymnast)
combat, combated, combatant
come back (*v.*), comeback (*n.*)
Come By Chance, N.L.
command, Maritime Command
commander (Cmdr. Wayne Elder)
    –lieutenant-commander (Lt.-Cmdr.)
    –wing commander (Wing Cmdr.)
commander-in-chief
commander of the Order of the British Empire
    (CBE)
commandment
    –the Ten Commandments
    –the Tenth Commandment
commando, commandos
command sergeant major
    –Command Sgt. Maj. Claude Laporte
commensurate
commiserate
Commission–Capitalize the proper name of
    government and royal commissions.
    –Commission on the Future of Health Care
    but the health-care commission
commitment
committal
committee
    –Commons finance committee
commodore (*no abbvn.*)
Common Prayer, Book of
common sense, a common-sense approach
Commons, House of

–the House, the Commons
commonwealth
 –the Commonwealth
 –Commonwealth of Australia
 –Commonwealth Development Bank
 –Commonwealth Games, the Games
 –Co-operative Commonwealth Federation
 (CCF)
communion, holy communion
 –Anglican communion
communism (philosophical attitude)
Communist (party, government or member)
 –anti-communist, non-communist,
 pro-communist
communist ideals (philosophical)
Companies' Creditors Arrangement Act (CCAA
 OK in second reference)
Company–Use Co. in business names.
 –American Broadcasting Cos. (ABC)
 –Brown Co.
 –*but* Canadian Opera Company
 (entertainment)
 –B Company (military)
company quartermaster-sergeant (*no abbvn.*)
company sergeant major (Company Sgt. Maj. John
 Jones)
 –company sergeants major
compare to (liken to), compare with (check
 similarities and differences)
compatible
compel, compelled, compelling
competent (*not* -ant)
complementary (serving to complete),
 complimentary (expressing compliment; free)
Computer Terms – *See Internet*
concede
concept, conception

–Immaculate Conception
concertgoer
concerto, concertos
Concorde (aircraft)
condole, condolence (*not* -ance)
Confederation (Canada)
    –Fathers of Confederation
Confederation of National Trade Unions (CNTU);
    in French, Conseil des syndicats nationaux
    (CSN)
conference
    –federal-provincial conference
    –Canada Conference (Evangelical)
    –Duke of Edinburgh's Study Conference
    –Law of the Sea conference
    –Conference Board of Canada
confidant (man), confidante (woman)
Confucian
Congo (formerly Zaire, formal name Democratic
    Republic of Congo)
Congo, Republic of (capital Brazzaville)
congregation
    –Congregation for the Doctrine of the
    Faith (Vatican)
Congress (U.S.)
    –*but* congressman, congressional
    –Senator John Smith (R-Tex.)
    –Representative Mary Smith (D-Mass.)
    –Congress party (India)
Congress of Racial Equality (CORE)
Connecticut (Conn.)
connoisseur (-nn-)
Connors, Stompin' Tom (singer-composer)
Conn Smythe Trophy (hockey)
conscientious
Conseil des syndicats nationaux (CSN); *but prefer*

Confederation of National Trade Unions
(CNTU)
consensus (*not* consensus of opinion)
Conservative (party), conservative (political
outlook)
–Conservative Party of Canada (formal
name)
–small-c conservative
constable (Const.)
–Const. Maria Huang
–a city constable
constitution, the French Constitution, the
constitution; *but* the Constitution (capped in
all references to Canada)
consulate, French Consulate, the consulate
consul general, Consul General Guy Tremblay
consumer price index (CPI, *but avoid*)
Consumers' Association of Canada
consummate
contact (*v.*, *adj.* and *n.*)
Contadora (island near Panama)
Continent, the (Europe)
continental shelf
contralto, contraltos
controller (*no abbvn.*)
–Controller Gillian Towers
convener (*not* -or)
converter (*not* -or)
cookbook
Cool TV (specialty channel)
Coon Come, Matthew (Coon Come *in second
reference*)
co-operate, co-operation
Co-operative Commonwealth Federation (CCF)
co-ordinate
copy editing, copy editor

copyright
  –Copyright, The Canadian Press
CORE (for Congress of Racial Equality)
co-respondent (divorce), correspondent (writer)
cornea (*sing.*), corneas (*pl.*)
Corner Brook, N.L.
Corner Brook Western Star
cornerstone, lay
Cornwall Standard-Freeholder
coronavirus (*one word*)
corporal (Cpl. Jane Smith)
  –lance-corporal (Lance-Cpl.)
Corporation–Use Corp. in business names.
  –Eastman Kodak Corp.
  –British Broadcasting Corp. (BBC)
  –Canadian Broadcasting Corp. (*but* CBC
  preferred)
corral, corralled
Correctional Service Canada, correctional
  service
cosy (*not* cozy)
council, city or county council, Peel regional
  council *but* Canada Council, Quebec Forest
  Industry Council, Council of Atlantic
  Premiers
councillor (Coun.)
  –Coun. Robert Jones
  –a city councillor
Council of Yukon First Nations
counsel, Crown counsel, Queen's counsel (QC, *but*
  avoid)
counsellor
counter-attack, counter-intelligence,
  counter-proposal, counterterrorism
countrywide
County–Capitalize when preceding or following a

specific term.
–Huron County
–County Derry
–*but* in the county of Huron
coureur de bois, coureurs de bois
Court–Capitalize superior courts but not lower
    courts.
    –Admiralty Court
    –Appeal Court
    –Court of Queen's Bench
    –European Court of Justice
    –family court
    –Federal Court, Federal Appeal Court
    –judicial committee of the Privy Council
    –Ontario court of justice (lower court)
    –provincial court
    –small claims court
    –Superior Court (Que.)
    –Superior Court of Justice (Ontario)
    –Supreme Court (fed., prov., state)
    –Tax Court (Canada, U.S.)
    –territorial court (N.W.T.)
    –U.S. Court of Appeals
    –U.S. Court of Military Appeals
    –youth court
    –the court ordered
Courtenay, B.C.
courthouse, courtroom
court martial, courts martial (*n.*), court-martial (*v.*)
Court of St. James's
CourtTV Canada (specialty channel)
Covent Garden (*not* Gardens)
cover up (*v.*), coverup (*n.*)
CPR – *See Canadian Pacific*
craftman (*no abbvn.*)
    –Craftman Elwood Greene (military)

--*but* craftsman (artisan)

Craigellachie, B.C. (where Last Spike was driven in railway in 1885)

creditor (one owed a debt; *not* -er)

Cree (*sing.* and *pl.*)

crescent (Cres.)

Crête, Paul (politician)

Creutzfeldt-Jakob disease (human spongiform encephalopathy; CJD OK *but explain*)

--variant Creutzfeldt-Jakob disease (variant CJD; the form related to mad cow disease)

crewman, crewwoman, crew member

cricket

--England-Australia Test match

--the Test

--the Ashes

Crime Stoppers (*two words*)

Criminal Code, the code

crisis, crises

criterion, criteria

criticism, criticize (*not* -ise)

Croat(s) (*n.*), Croatian (*adj.*)

CROP Inc. (Centre de recherches sur l'opinion publique; Quebec-based polling firm)

cross-border

cross-checking

cross-country

cross-examine, cross-examination

crossfire

Crow, Sheryl (singer)

crown

--the Crown (judge or prosecutor)

--the Crown alleges ...

--Crown attorney, counsel

--Crown attorney Liz Baker

--a Crown corporation, Crown land

    −a crown prince
    −*but* Crown Prince Rupert
Crowsnest Pass
Crucifixion
cruise (missile)
Crusades
crybaby (*no hyphen*), crybabies
CSeries jet (Bombardier)
CT scan (computerized tomography)
CTV Newsnet
cubism, cubist
Cultural Revolution (China)
cummings, e.e. (1894-1962)
cup, Stanley Cup (trophy)
        −America's Cup (yachting)
        −Canada Cup (hockey)
        −Canada's Cup (yachting)
cupful, cupfuls
Curia (Vatican office)
Curling−bonspiel, free-guard zone, hog line,
        in-turn draw, out-turn draw, shot rock
curriculum, curricula
curtain, Iron Curtain
curtsy, curtsies
CUSO (OK *in first reference*, originally stood for
        Canadian University Service Overseas)
customs, Canada Customs
        −a customs officer
        −go through customs
cyberspace
cyclosporine
cystic fibrosis
czar, Czar Nicholas
Czech Republic

D

dachshund

Dacotah, Man.

Dacron (trademark for polyester fibre)

Dahomey (Benin since 1975)

DaimlerChrysler

Dalai Lama, the

Dalmatian

dame, Dame Maggie Smith (*but avoid*),
> Smith (*second reference*)

damn, damned, damn it, God damn

Dances–Lowercase names.
> –break dancing, bump, charleston, foxtrot,
> go-go, minuet, pas de deux, polka,
> polonaise, twist

danish (pastry)

Dar es Salaam
> –DAR ES SALAAM (in placelines)

Dari (language dominant in Afghanistan)

Dark Ages

Dash 8

data (*plural*)

databank, database

dateline, placeline
> –*but* international date line

Dates–Write December 2004 without commas and
> Dec. 14, 2004, with commas. In dates,
> abbreviate the months except March, April,
> May, June and July: Aug. 1, May 3. Write
> Christmas 2005.
> –1997-98 but 1999-2002

da Vinci – *See Leonardo*

Day–Capitalize religious holidays and feasts and
> all special times.
> –All Saints' Day
> –Christmas Eve
> –Earth Day

–*but* election day
day care *but* day-care centre
daylight (*not* daylight saving) time
    –ADT, EDT, etc.
daylong (*one word*)
day trader
D-Day (June 6, 1944)
DDT (dichlorodiphenyltrichloroethane)
de, der, di, du, d'–When lowercase in names,
    capitalize only at start of sentence.
    –de Gaulle, Charles
    –de Havilland Inc. (division of Bombardier
    Inc.)
    –De Laurentiis, Dino (movies)
    –deMille, Cecil B. (movies)
    –deWit, Willie (boxing)
    –de facto (two words – existing, whether legal or
    not)
    –de jure (two words – by right, by law; *but*
    avoid)
    –deluxe (*one word*)
    –de rigueur (*not* -geur)
de- (*prefix*), deactivate, debar, decompress,
    de-emphasize, de-escalate, defrost, de-ice,
    de-ink, deodorize, destabilize
dean, dean of arts
debacle
debonair
deceive, deceivable (*not* -eable), deceiver
decision-making
-decker, double-decker
Decorations–Capitalize specific names.
    –Distinguished Service Cross (DSC)
decrepit
deductible (*not* -able)
deejay – *Use* DJ

D

deepsea (*adj.*, *no hyphen*)

Deep South (U.S.)

defence (*not* defense), *but* defensive

defenceman (*one word*)

defuse (remove fuse), diffuse (spread)

Degrees–Lowercase college and other degrees
     unless abbreviated. *See University Degrees*

Deja View (specialty TV channel)

Delaware (Del.)

delicatessen

delta, Mekong River Delta

demagogue, demagogy (*not* -goguery)

demeanour

Democrat
     –Representative Mary Smith (D–Texas)
     –Senator John Smith (D–Mass.)

Democratic party (U.S.)
     –New Democratic Party (NDP)
     –a New Democrat

Dene (pronounced Den'-neh)
     –Dene Nation (represents aboriginals in
     Northwest Territories)

Denendeh (Dene name for Northwest Territories)

Deng Xiaoping, Deng (1904-1997)

Departments–Capitalize international, national
     and provincial government departments and
     ministries. Lowercase municipal, school and
     business departments.
     –Department of National Defence
     –Defence Department
     –Department of Indian and Northern Affairs
     –Indian Affairs Department
     –Vietnam Health Ministry
    Lowercase department in plural uses.
     –the Defence and Industry departments
    Capitalize the proper-name element when

standing alone and used as noun meaning the department.

–She went to Defence from Industry.

–*but* Toronto parks department

–McGill history department

It is not necessary to use the full formal name of a department if a shorter version is clear: Fisheries Department, *not* Department of Fisheries and Oceans or Fisheries and Oceans Canada.

dependant (*n.*), dependent (*adj.*), dependence (*not* -ance)

deprecate (disapprove), depreciate (belittle, lose value)

Depression (or Great Depression), the (1930s)

deputy

–Deputy Prime Minister Linda Graves, Deputy Chief Joe Jones (formal title)

–deputy premier Saul Hillier (informal position)

–deputy Speaker Jean Turcotte

–the deputy Speaker

–deputy Crown attorney Alys Yamata

de rigueur (*not* riguer)

descendant (offspring)

descendent (descending)

-designate, prime minister-designate John Block, the chairman-designate

desirable (*not* -eable)

Desjarlais, Bev (politician)

desktop *(one word)*

desperate, desperation

despoliation (*not* despoilation)

detective

–Det. Fred Lisak (police)

–private detective James Brown

D

deterrent (*not* -ant)
Deutsche Grammophon (recordings)
Deutschmark (*prefer* German mark)
DeVillers, Paul (politician)
Devoir, Le (Montreal newspaper)
devotee
DEW (for Distant Early Warning) Line
Dhaka, Bangladesh
Dhalla, Ruby (politician)
dialed, dialing
dial up (*v.*), dial-up (*adj., n.*)
dialysis
diameter
Diana, or Princess of Wales (*not* Princess Diana)
diaphragm
diarrhea
DiCaprio, Leonardo (actor)
Dickensian
Dictaphone (trademark for a dictation recorder)
die, dying
Diefenbaker, John (1895-1979)
diehard
Diet (national legislative body)
dietitian
diffuse (spread), defuse (remove fuse)
dike (barrier; *not* dyke)
dilemma
dilettante, dilettantes
DiMaggio, Joe (1914-1999)
dining room
diocese, Hamilton diocese
Dion, Stéphane
diphtheria
diphthong
disaster, disastrous
disc, compact disc (CD, CD-ROM), slipped disc,

disc brake, disc jockey *but* floppy disk,
    diskette
discernible (*not* -able)
discolour
Discovery Channel, the (TV)
discreet (circumspect), discrete (separate, abstract)
disease, legionnaires' disease, Minamata disease
dishonour
disingenuous (insincere)
disinterested (impartial), uninterested (not
    interested)
dispel, dispelled
dissension (*not* -tion)
dissociate (*not* disassociate)
distil, distiller
Distinguished Service Cross (DSC)
district attorney, district attorney Mike Fuhrmann
Ditto (trademark for copier)
dived (*not* dove)
divisibility, divisible, divisive
division, 6th Division
divorcée (woman; *avoid*)
DJ (*not* deejay), DJs, DJing, DJed
DNA (deoxyribonucleic acid)
Dobson, Fefe (singer)
doctor (Dr., *but avoid* unless health-care
    professional)
    –doctor of laws (LLD)
    –doctor of medicine (MD)
    –doctor of philosophy (PhD)
docudrama
Dofasco Inc. (formerly Dominion Foundries and
    Steel Corp.)
dogcatcher, dogfight, doghouse, dog-tag
Dogs–Capitalize breed names derived from proper
    names except where usage has established
    the lowercase.

-Dalmatian
-Doberman pinscher
-German shepherd
-Newfoundland, Great Dane
-St. Bernard, Irish terrier
-*but* alsatian, dachshund, collie, pekinese, spaniel, etc.
Dominica (small Caribbean island republic)
Dominican Republic (neighbour of Haiti)
dominion
-Dominion of Canada
domino, dominoes
Domtar Inc.
donegal tweed
-*but* County Donegal
Donnybrook (town), donnybrook (riot)
dos and don'ts
Dosanjh, Ujjal (politician)
Dostoyevsky, Fyodor (novelist, 1821-1881)
dot-com (company, millionaire, etc.)
double-A-plus, double-A-minus (bonds)
doublecross, doublecrosser
double-decker
doubleheader (*one word*)
doubletalk
doughnut (*never* donut except in corporate names)
Doukhobor
Dow Jones (*no hyphen*)
-Dow Jones Canada
-Dow Jones industrial average, Dow Jones industrials
Down East
downhill
down payment (*two words*)
Down syndrome
-Down Syndrome Association of Canada

D

Downtown Eastside (Vancouver)
Down Under (Australia and New Zealand)
Doyle, Damhnait (singer)
D'Oyly Carte
draconian
draegerman (mine-rescue worker)
draft (air, money, plan, military, beer)
draftsman
Dragon (sailboat)
Dramamine (trademark for travel-sickness
    medicine)
dreck
dressing room (*two words*)
drive (Dr.)
    –111 Sutherland Dr.
    –*but* 24 Sussex Drive (official residence)
driver's licence
drive in (*v.*), drive-in (*n.*), drive-thru (*n.*)
Droit, Le (Ottawa-Gatineau newspaper)
drop-down (*adj.*), drop-down menu
drop out (*v.*), dropout (*n.*)
drugstore (*one word*)
dry, drier, driest
    –*but* hair, laundry dryer
Dubai
duchess
    –Duchess of Cornwall (formerly Camilla
    Parker Bowles)
Duesseldorf, Germany
duffel bag, coat
duke, Duke of Windsor
dumbfound
Dunkirk (*not* Dunkerque)
Dunlap, David Dunlap Observatory (near Toronto)
DuPont – See *E.I. du Pont Canada Co.*
durum wheat

D

Dutoit, Charles (conductor)
DVD (for digital video disc; *OK in first reference*)
dwarf, dwarfs
dye, dyeing
dynamo, dynamos
dysentery
dysfunction
dyslexia

earl, Earl Spencer
  –Earl of Athlone
Earth–Capitalize when referred to as a planet.
  –The planets nearest the sun are Mercury,
  Venus and Earth.
  –The astronauts turned back to Earth.
  –down to earth
  –the good earth
  –heaven on earth
East–Capitalize regions *but not* their derivatives.
  Lowercase mere direction or position.
  –the East (region)
  –an easterner
  –Eastern Canada
  –an eastern Canadian
  –eastern Canadian markets
  –The snow moved east over Eastern Canada.
  –in eastern Quebec
  –East Coast (region)
  –east coast (shoreline)
  –where East meets West
  –eastern nations
  –eastern Europe (no longer a bloc)
  –Eastern Hemisphere
  –the Far East
East Block (Ottawa)
Eastern Townships (Quebec)
East India, East Indian – *Use* South Asia, South
    Asian
Eaton's (T. Eaton Co. Ltd., now defunct)
EBay (*not* eBay)
Ebola virus
echo, echoes
E. coli (bacteria)
e-commerce
ecstasy (*lowercase*) (*OK in first reference* for

methylenedioxymethamphetamine)
ecumenical council
eczema
Edmonton Road Runners (AHL)
Edmundston, N.B.
EDT (*not* EDST)
educator (*prefer* teacher)
effect (*n.* – result); (*v.* – bring about)
effrontery (shameless insolence), affront (deliberate
    insult)
e.g. (exempli gratia; *avoid*)
Eglin (*not* Elgin) Field, Fla.
Egoyan, Atom (film director)
E.I. du Pont Canada Co.
    –DuPont (U.S.)
    –Samuel F. Du Pont (his usage)
Eiffel Tower (Paris)
Eilat (Israeli port)
Einstein, Albert (1879-1955)
El ("the")–ln Arabic names of individuals, the
    articles el and al may be used or dropped
    depending on the person's preference or
    established usage: Osama el-Baz, el-Baz
    (*second reference*); *but* Moammar Gadhafi,
    Gadhafi.
   For other names, the article is usually
    uppercase: Bordj El Kiffan (city in Algeria)
-elect, president-elect George W. Bush
    –*but* prime minister-designate Jean Chrétien
election day
Elections Canada
Elizabeth Fry Society
Elliot Lake, Ont. (*one t*)
ellipsis, ellipses
Elysée Palace
e-mail, electronic mail

embargo, embargoes
embarrass, embarrassment
embassy, Canadian Embassy, Ukrainian Embassy,
    the embassy
embryo, embryos
emcee – *Use* MC
Emergis Inc. (TSX:EME)
emeritus
    –Jean Duval, professor emeritus of history
emigrant, emigrate, emigration
Emmy, Emmys (TV awards)
emphysema
empire
    –British Commonwealth and Empire, the
    Empire
    –Holy Roman Empire
Empire State Building
employment insurance (*no caps*), EI (*second
    reference)*
enamour, enamoured (of)
EnCana Corp. (formerly Alberta Energy Co. and
    PanCanadian Energy; TSX:ECA)
encyclopedia
    –*but* Encyclopaedia Britannica
endeavour
Energy Board, National (NEB, *but avoid)*
Engel, Marian (writer, 1933-1985)
England–Do not abbreviate and do not use as
    synonym for Britain.
English Canada, English-Canadian
enormity (wickedness), enormousness (size)
Enquirer, Cincinnati (newspaper)
enquiry – *Use* inquiry
enrol (*not* enroll), enrolled, enrolment
en route (*always two words*)
ensign (rank, *no abbvn.*)

E

ensign, the Red Ensign
ensure (make sure of)
entomological, entomologist, entomology
entrepreneur, entrepreneurial
Environmental Protection Agency (EPA, *but avoid*)
epigram (witty saying), epitaph (inscription on a
     tomb), epithet (descriptive word or phrase)
equator
Erasmus, Georges
Erickson, Arthur (architect)
Ericsson, Leif (Viking, about 970 -1020)
erratum, errata
Eskasoni (Cape Breton First Nations band)
esker (post-glacial gravel)
Eskimo, Eskimos, *but use* Inuk, Inuit
Eskimo Point – *See Arviat, Nunavut*
ESL (English as a second language; *explain*)
Esquimalt, B.C.
esthete, esthetic
Eternal City
ethnic-Albanian (*adj.*)
eucharist (holy communion)
euro(s) (EU currency), eight euros, 8.1 euros, 26
     euros
Eurodollar (*no hyphen*)
European Court of Justice
European Parliament (legislative body of EU)
European Union (EU)
euthanasia (*preferred to* mercy killing)
even-steven
everyday (*adj., one word*)
exaggerate, exaggeration
exhilarate
exhort
existence (*not* -ance)
existentialism

exonerate
exorbitant (*not* exhorbitant)
expedite, expediter (*not* -or)
expel, expelled
Expo 67, Expo 86 (*no apostrophe*)
extemporaneous (*not* -eraneous)
Extendicare Inc. (TSX:EXE.MV)
extra-bill (*v.*), extra-billing (*n.*)
extracurricular
extraterritorial (*no hyphen*)
extravagant (*not* -ent)
Exxon Corp.
eye, eyeball, eyebrow, eyeful, eyeing, eyelash,
        eyelid, eyesight, eyesore, eyewitness (*no
        hyphens*)
e-zine (Internet magazine)

face off (*v.*), faceoff (*n.*)

faculty, faculty of law

FA Cup (Football Association Cup)
    –the Cup competition

Fahd Ibn Abdul Aziz (Saudi Arabia)
    –King Fahd *acceptable in first reference*

Fahrenheit, –20 F (dash, space before F, no period)

Fairbairn, Joyce (senator)

Fairmont Hotels & Resorts Inc. (TSX:FHR)

Falconbridge Ltd. (TSX:FL)

fall (season)

fallacious, fallacy

fallible, fallibility

Fallopian tube

fall out (*v.*), fallout (*n.*)

FAQ(s) (frequently asked question(s))

Far East

Far North

Farquharson, Charlie (character created by Don
    Harron)

fascism (philosophical attitude)

Fascist (party, member or government)

fascist trends

Father – *Use* Rev. as title for Catholic priest

Father's Day (third Sunday in June)

Fathers of Confederation

faux pas

favour, favourite, favourable

fax (*n.* and *v.*)

faze (disconcert), phase (stage)

federal
    –federal election
    –federal government

Federal Bureau of Investigation (FBI)

Federal Communications Commission (FCC, *but
    avoid*)

F

Federal Court
Federal Energy Administration (FEA, *but avoid*)
Federation of Canadian Municipalities (*no abbvn.*)
feedback (*n., no hyphen*)
feisty
fellow, fellowship
    –Nieman Fellowship
ferris wheel (*lowercase*)
fervour
fetal alcohol syndrome
Fête nationale (Quebec holiday on June 24, also
    St-Jean-Baptiste Day)
fettuccine
fetus (*not* foetus)
Feux follets, the (*no hyphen* – dance group)
fever, Lassa fever, spring fever
fiancé (man), fiancée (woman)
Fiberglas (trademark for fibreglass or glass fibre)
field, a polo field
    –Soldier Field
field marshal (*no abbvn.*)
fiery, fierier, fieriest
Fife wheat, Red Fife wheat
Fifth Estate, The (TV program)
fighter-bomber
Fig Newton (trademark for cookies)
Filion, Hervé (harness racing)
Filipino (male), Filipina (female), Filipinos
filmmaker
fiord
fire, fire department, firearm, firebrand, firebomb,
firecracker, firefighter, fireplace
first lady (U.S. president's wife, *but avoid*)
first lieutenant (1st Lieut.)
first ministers conference, meeting
First Nations

F

First World War (*not* World War I)
fivepins (bowling)
flack (press agent), flak (anti-aircraft fire)
Flags–Capitalize the names of flags and ensigns.
> –Fleur-de-lis, Maple Leaf, Red Ensign, Rising Sun, Stars and Stripes, Tricolour, Union Jack

flair (talent), flare (flame, widening)
flak (anti-aircraft fire), flack (press agent)
flamboyant (*no* u)
flamingo, flamingos
flammable (*prefer to* inflammable)
flare up (*v.*), flare-up (*n.*)
flatcar
flaunt (show off), flout (mock)
flavour
fleet
> –the U.S. fleet (whole navy)
> –U.S. Pacific Fleet (formation)
> –Fleet Air Arm (Royal Navy)

Fleming, Sir Sandford (1827-1915)
fleur-de-lis (*not* -lys), Fleur-de-lis (flag)
flexibility, flexible
Flight 132 (*capitalize*)
flight lieutenant (Flight Lieut.)
flight sergeant (Flight Sgt.)
floe (floating sheet of ice)
Florida (Fla.)
flotation (*not* float-)
flounder (thrash about), founder (sink)
flout (mock), flaunt (show off)
FLQ (Front de libération du Québec)
flu (*no apostrophe*)
flutist
flyer (*not* flier), fly-fishing, flyleaf, flypast, fly swatter (*two words*), flyweight, flywheel,
frequent flyer

F

Flying Dutchman (sailboat)
flying officer (*no abbvn.*)
FM (frequency modulation)
FN (for Fabrique nationale) rifle
focus, focused, focuses, focusing
folksinger, folksong
followup (*n.* and *adj.*)
Food and Drugs (*not* Drug) Act
foofaraw
foot-and-mouth disease (*not* hoof-)
Football–backup centre, ball carrier, ball club, blitz
    (*n., v.*), bootleg, end line, end zone, field goal,
    fourth-and-one (*adj.*), fullback, goal-line,
    goal-line stand, halfback, halftime, handoff,
    kick off (*v.*), kickoff (*n., adj.*), left guard,
    linebacker, lineman, nose tackle, out of
    bounds (*adv.*), out-of-bounds (*adj.*), pitchout
    (*n.*), place kick, placekicker, play off (*v.*),
    playoff (*n., adj.*), quarterback, runback (*n.*),
    running back, tailback, tight end, touchback,
    touchdown
forbear (refrain from), forbearance; forebear
    (ancestor)
force-feeding
Forces, the; Canadian Forces; the Forces (capped
    for Canadian only)
forego (precede), foregone; forgo (go without),
    forgone
Foreign Legion
Foreign Office (U.K.)
forerunner
foresaw, foresee, foreseeable, foreseen
foreword (in a book)
forfeit, forfeiture
forgivable (*not* -eable), forgive

forgo (go without), forgone; forego (precede), foregone

format

former
    –former King (Canada, U.K.)
    –former king (other nations)
    –former president George Bush
    –former prime minister Brian Mulroney
    –former Speaker John Fraser
    –former senator Robert de Cotret

Formica (trademark for a laminated plastic)

formula, formulas

Formula One (auto racing), F1 (*OK in second reference*)

Forrester, Maureen (contralto)

Fort Chimo, Que. – *See Kuujjuaq*

Fort Chipewyan, Alta.

Fort Frances, Ont.

Fort Macleod, Alta.

Fort McMurray, Alta.

Fort Qu'Appelle, Sask.

Fortran (for formula translation)

founder (sink), flounder (thrash about)

Four Seasons Hotels Inc. (TSX:FSH.SV)

Fourth Estate (press)

Fourth of July, July Fourth (U.S. holiday)

foxtrot (*one word*)

fracas

francization (*not* -isation – *but preferably avoid*)

Franco-Manitoban

Franco-Ontarian

francophone (*lowercase*)

Francophonie, la (French-speaking equivalent of the Commonwealth)

freebie (free trip or other benefit)

freelance (*n.*, *v.* and *adj.*); freelancer (*n.*)

F

Freemason (*one word*)
freestyle swimming
french bread, french door, french fries, french-fried
      potatoes
French Canada, French-Canadian
      –French-speaking Canadian
French Revolution
frequency modulation (FM)
fresco, frescoes
Freudian
Friedan, Betty (feminist)
Frigidaire (trademark for appliances)
Frisbee (trade name)
Frobisher Bay – *Use* Iqaluit, Nunavut
Front, the (off Newfoundland)
Front de libération du Québec (FLQ)
front man *(two words)*
front-runner
Frulla, Liza (politician)
Fry, Elizabeth Fry Society
Fry, Hedy (politician)
Frye, Northrop (scholar, 1912-1991)
FTP (for file transfer protocol)
fuck – *Avoid* with few exceptions. (See *Stylebook*,
      page 18.) Use full word, not f*** or F-word.
      F-word is used if said that way in a quote.
Fudgsicle (trademark)
fuel, fuelled, fuelling, fuel cell, fuel injection
Fuehrer, the (leader; used by Adolf Hitler)
-ful *(suffix)*, boxful, careful, cheerful, cupful(s),
      handful(s), harmful, spoonful(s), thoughtful,
      useful
fulfil (*not* fulfill), fulfilled, fulfilment
full time, a full-time job, working full time
fulsome (pejorative term, meaning excessive)
fundraiser, fundraising, fundraise

F

fungus, fungi
furor (*not* furore)
fusilier (*no abbvn.*)
　　–Fusilier Georges Coté
futile, futilely, futility
FX (movie special effects; spell out *in first reference*)

Gadhafi, Moammar
gaff (spar; fish-landing stick); gaffe (faux pas)
Gagliano, Alfonso (politician)
Gagnon, Christiane (politician)
gaiety
Gallup poll
Game Boy (video game)
Gandhi (*not* Ghandi)
garnishee (*v.* – preferable to garnish)
Gap (retailer)
Gastown (in downtown Vancouver)
Gatineau, Que. (formerly Hull)
GATT (General Agreement on Tariffs and Trade)
gaucho, gauchos
gauge
gauntlet (*not* gantlet)
Gaza Strip
gefilte fish
geiger counter
Geiger-Torel, Herman (opera)
genealogist
general (Gen.)
> –chief of the general staff
> –Gen. Charles de Gaulle
> –Gen. William Worth

General–In compounds, hyphenate general when it
> is the key word: major-general. Otherwise:
> attorney general, auditor general, governor
> general, secretary general.

General Agreement on Tariffs and Trade (GATT)
General Assembly (of UN)
> –*but* general assembly of the United Church

generation X, generation Xers
genetically modified (GM, *but avoid*)
Genghis Khan (c. 1162-1227)
Genie (movie award)

G

genius, geniuses

gentile

genus, genera

Geographical Terms–Capitalize regions but not mere direction or position. Capitalize Lake, River, Mountain, Strait, County, etc., when preceding or following the specific term; *but* lowercase the common-noun part of names in plural uses: Ottawa and St. Lawrence rivers, lakes Huron and Superior.

George Cross (GC), Medal (GM)

Georges Bank (fishing)

George Town (Bahamas, Malaysia, Tasmania –most others are Georgetown, *but* check)

George Weston Ltd. (TSX:WN)

Georgia (Ga.)

germane

German measles

Germany, Germanys

Gerussi, Bruno (actor, 1928-1995)

get together (*v.*), get-together (*n.*)

Ghanaian

ghetto, ghettos

ghoul, ghoulish

Gielgud, Sir John (actor, 1904-2000)

gigabyte (GB – *sing.* and *pl.* metric symbol)

gigahertz (GHz; *avoid or include explanation*: one billion cycles a second)

gigolo, gigolos

girlfriend, boyfriend

Girl Guides of Canada (association)
>   –a girl guide, a guide
>   –the Girl Guides, the Guides (association)
>   –the Girl Guides movement
>   –Brownie
>   –Spark
>   –Pathfinder

Gitxsan-Wet'suwet'en
Giuseppe (Italian for Joseph)
gizmo, gizmos
gladiolus, gladioli
glamour (*but* glamorous, glamorize)
glasnost
global positioning system (*lowercase; GPS OK in second reference*)
Globe and Mail, the Globe and Mail
   –in bylines only, *uppercase* the:
    By Greg Keenan
    The Globe and Mail
GNP (gross national product)
goalkeeper, goalmouth, goalpost, goaltender (*one word*), *but* goal-line (hyphen)
gobbledygook
god (idol)
God–Capitalize sacred names and the proper names and nicknames of the devil: God, Allah, Yahweh, the Almighty, the Father, Jesus Christ, the Son, the Lamb of God, the Saviour, our Lord, Holy Spirit, Trinity, the Prophet (Muhammad), Virgin Mary, Archangel Michael, Angel Gabriel, Satan, Lucifer, Old Nick.
   Capitalize He, Him, His, Thou, Thee, Thine, You, Your in reference to the Deity. But lowercase who, whom, whose.
godchild, godfather, godmother
God damn, God damned (*not* goddam) – *Use with discretion.*
godsend
Gods Lake, Man.
Goebbels, Josef (1897-1945)
Goering, Hermann (1893-1946)
gofer

G

go-go
goitre
Golden Horseshoe (Oshawa to St. Catharines, Ont.)
Golf–birdie (1 under par), bogey (1 over par; bogeys,
bogeyed), double bogey, triple-bogey 7, eagle
(2 under par), par 4, par-4 hole, three-wood,
No. 3 wood, 1 over par for the round, shot a 1-
over-par 73, the Bell Canadian Open (men).
BMO Financial Group Canadian Women's
Open, Canadian Professional Golfers'
Association (CPGA), the Canadian Tour, Ladies
Professional Golf Association (LPGA), Masters
tournament, PGA Tour, Royal Canadian Golf
Association (RCGA), Champions Tour (senior
PGA tour)
gonif (thief; clever person; prankster)
gonorrhea
goodbye (*no hyphen*)
Good Friday
Good Samaritan
goodwill (*n.* and *adj.*)
Google, Googled, Googling (*uppercase*)
GOP (U.S. Republican party, *but avoid*)
gorilla
Gortex (trademark for fabric)
gospel, the Four Gospels
–the Gospels
–the Gospel of St. Luke
–the gospel truth
–a gospel singer
got (*not* gotten)
Goteborg (*not* Gothenburg)
Gothic (architectural style) *but* a gothic novel
GO Transit, GO train (for Government of Ontario)
Gouk, Jim (politician)
Gould, Glenn (pianist, 1932-1982)
Gouzenko, Igor (Soviet defector, 1919-1982)

Government–Capitalize national legislative bodies, including some short forms.
–House of Commons, Commons
–House of Lords, Lords
–House of Representatives, House
–Bundestag, Diet, Knesset
Lowercase provincial legislatures and their equivalents and county or city councils.
–Manitoba legislature
–Quebec national assembly
–Toronto city council
governor, governor-in-council (cabinet)
–Gov. Julius Mason
–former governor Anne Lewcyk
–Bank of Canada governor David Dodge
Governor General–Capitalize in all references to the Canadian incumbent; otherwise only as a title preceding a name.
–Gov. Gen. Adrienne Clarkson
–the Governor General (Canada)
–the governor general (others)
–former governor general Ed Schreyer
–governors general (*pl.*)
–Governor General's Awards, Governor General's Award for poetry
(*never* GG or GGs)
–Governor General's Horse Guards, Governor General's Foot Guards
Grade 7 – *Use* numerals; *but* seventh grade
graffito, graffiti
Graham, Alasdair (senator)
Graham, Katharine (Washington Post, 1917-2001)
Grain–Capitalize variety names generally except where usage has established the lowercase.
–Thatcher, Selkirk, Rescue
–*but* durum, garnet, Alberta red winter,
No. 1 northern

grain grower
grain handler
Grammy, Grammys (record awards)
Granada (Spanish city), Grenada (island in the
     Caribbean)
Grand Canyon
granddaughter, great-granddaughter
Grande Prairie, Alta.
Grande Prairie Herald-Tribune
grand jury
grandmaster (bridge and chess)
Grand Prix racing
     –Canadian Grand Prix auto race
Grands ballets canadiens, les; les Grands
grassroots (*one word*)
Gray, Herb (chair, International Joint Commission)
Greater Toronto Area (Toronto and surrounding
     urban regions; GTA *but avoid*)
great-grandfather, great-grandmother
Great-West Lifeco Inc. (TSX:GWO)
Green Berets
Greene, Graham (novelist, 1904-1991)
Greene, Lorne (actor, 1915-1987)
Greenly Island
green movement (environmentalists); Green party
green paper (a tentative report of government
     proposals)
Greenpeace Foundation
     –Greenpeace V (vessel)
Greenwich Village
Greer, Germaine (feminist)
Grenada (island in the Caribbean), Granada (Spanish
     city)
Grenfell, Sir Wilfred (1865-1940)
Gretzky, Wayne
Grewal, Gurmant (politician)

grey (colour)
Grey Cup (football)
Grey, Deborah (politician)
Grey, Earl (governor general, Grey Cup)
Grey, Earle (arts award)
Grey Panthers
grey whale
grippe
grisly (gruesome), grizzly (bear)
Grit (Liberal)
gross domestic product (GDP)
gross national product (GNP)
groundcrew (aviation – *one word)*
Groundhog Day (Feb. 2)
groundswell (*one word*)
Ground Zero (New York City), ground zero (other uses)
group captain (Group Capt. Ed Moir)
Group of Seven (artists), G7, G8 (countries)
grown-up (*n.* and *adj.*)
GST (*acceptable in first reference* for goods and services tax)
guacamole
guardsman (*no abbvn.; but* coastguardman)
guerrilla
guide, a girl guide
   –Girl Guides of Canada (association)
   –the Guides
Guinness (stout)
   –Arthur Guinness, Son and Co. (Dublin) Ltd.
   –Guinness World Records
Guinness, Sir Alec (1914-2000)
Gulf of Aqaba
Gulf Stream
gun, Bren gun, Sten gun
gunfight

gung-ho

gunner (*no abbvn.*)

gunnery sergeant (Gunnery Sgt.)

Guns–Rifles, pistols and other small arms are usually described in calibre, expressed in decimal fractions of an inch or in metric. The word calibre is not used with metric measurements. Shotguns are measured in gauge.

–M-16 rifle, 75-mm gun, 12-gauge shotgun, .410-bore shotgun, .45-calibre automatic, 30-30 rifle, .22-calibre rifle

gunship

gunwale

Gurkha (*not* Ghurka)

gurney

guttural (*not* -eral)

Gwich'in (aboriginal band)

gynecologist, gynecology

Gypsy, Gypsies (race of nomadic peoples; also called Roma)

–*but* gypsy moth, gypsy cab

Gzowski, Peter (broadcaster, 1934-2002)

H–Four words and their derivatives begin with silent "h" – heir, honest, honour and hour – requiring "an": an honest man. Otherwise: a historic battle, a hotel.

Haagen-Dazs (ice cream)

habeas corpus (writ)

Habsburg (*not* Hapsburg) Empire

Hague, The

Haida (*sing.* and *pl.*)

Haidasz, Stanley (senator)

hail, hailstone, hailstorm

Hailey, Arthur (novelist)

hair's-breadth

hajj (Muslim pilgrimage)

hakapik (club used in seal hunt)

half, one-half
> –half a dozen
> –a half-dozen

half-, halfback, half-baked, half-hour, half-mast, halftime, halftone (engraving), halves (*pl.*), halfway, halfwit, halfwitted

half-mast (*not* half-staff)

Halifax Chronicle-Herald

Halifax Daily News

Halifax Mail-Star

Haligonian (resident of Halifax)

hall, city hall, firehall
> –Massey Hall
> –Roy Thomson Hall
> –Toronto City Hall

Halley's comet

Hall, Monty

Hall of Fame

Halloween (*no apostrophe*)

Hamburger Helper (trademark for dinner mix)

Hamilton (specify if not Ontario)

Hamilton Tiger-Cats (*but* Ticats)

handcuff (*v.*), handcuffs (*pl. n.*)

Handel, George Frideric (composer, 1685-1759)

handful, handfuls

hand-held (*n.* and *adj.*)

handmade

H&R Block Ltd. (*no periods*; *no spaces*)

handshake (*no hyphen*)

hangar (aircraft), hanger (clothes, etc.)

Hanger, Art (politician)

Hannover, Germany

Hanukkah

Hapsburg – *Use* Habsburg

hara-kiri

harass, harassing, harassment

harbour, Victoria harbour

hard line, hardline policy, hardliner

harebrained

Hare Krishna, Hare Krishnas

HarperCollins Canada Ltd. (publishers)

Harper's Magazine

Harris, Lawren (painter, 1885-1970)

Harrods (London store)

Hart Memorial Trophy, Hart Trophy (hockey)

hat trick

Havel, Vaclav

Hawaii (*no abbvn.*), Hawaiian

Hawker Siddeley Canada Inc.

H-bomb

Headingley, Man.

Headlines–The usual CP rules for text apply, with the following changes to help keep headlines short:

Abbreviations: Allowed in all uses for all Canadian provinces and territories except Yukon and Nunavut. Other well-known

abbreviations can be used (StatsCan for
Statistics Canada, etc.) as a last resort if
length is an issue.

For numbers under 10, use numerals (8 instead
of eight).

Symbols: Use % instead of per cent. Use M for
million, but only after a numeral ($2M in
funding). Q1, Q2, etc., permitted for first
quarter, second quarter in business headlines.

Quotation marks: Use single, not double marks.
Capitalize the first word only, unless headline
is in body of story, when all principal words
are capped.

headquarters (*usually takes a plural verb*)

Heads–Capitalize principal words in headings of
tables, lists and other tabular matter.

health care (*n.*) health-care (*adj.*)

hearsay

hearse

heat wave (*two words*)

heaven

heavy water

Hec Crighton Trophy

Hegira, the (Muhammad's)

Heimlich manoeuvre

helix, helixes

hell

Hello (*not* Hello!) magazine

Hells Angels (*no apostrophe*), Angels (*second
reference*)

helter-skelter

hemisphere
–Western Hemisphere

hemophilia

hemorrhage

Hennessy, Jill (actor)

H

hepatitis A, B, C
herculean (*lowercase*)
Her Majesty–*See His*
hero, heroes (*pl.*)
heyday (*no hyphen*)
Hezbollah (Party of God)
hiccup, hiccuped
hide-and-seek, hideaway, hideout
hieroglyph, hieroglyphs (*n.*); hieroglyphic (*adj.*),
     hieroglyphics (*n., pl.*)
High Arctic
highbrow (*no hyphen*)
high commissioner, High Commissioner Lauren
     Chow
highlight (*no hyphen*)
high mass
highrise
high-tech
highway
     –the highway to Paris
     –Highway 27
     –Trans-Canada Highway
hijab
Hill, the (informal for Parliament Hill)
hindrance
Hindu, Hinduism
hip hop (*n.*), hip-hop music (*adj.*)
hippie, hippies
hippopotamus, hippopotamuses
Hirsch, John (1930-1989)
His–Capitalize His in reference to the Deity, His (or
     Her) Majesty, His (or Her) Royal Highness,
     His Holiness, His Grace, His Honour, His
     Lordship, His Worship. But use such terms of
     address only in quotations.
     –His Worship Mayor Phillips

–and His Worship said ...

–His Royal Highness, the Prince of Wales

Hispanic

historic (important or outstanding in history)

    –historical (about history)

    –a (*not* an) historical site

Historical Eras–Capitalize historical periods and events, including widely recognized popular names: Pliocene Epoch, Stone Age, Iron Age, Exodus, Ming Dynasty, Dark Ages, Middle Ages, Hundred Years War, Renaissance, American Civil War, Prohibition, Great Depression, Roaring '20s, Dirty '30s, Beer Hall Putsch, Holocaust, Space Age, Me Decade; *but* ice age (no single period)

    –21st century

History Television (specialty TV channel))

hitchhike, hitchhiking (*no hyphen*)

Hitler, Adolf (*not* Adolph) (1889-1945)

HIV (for human immunodeficiency virus)

    –HIV-positive

Ho Chi Minh (North Vietnam), Ho Chi Minh Trail

Hockey–blue-line, face off (*v.*), faceoff (*n., adj.*), goalie, goal-line, goalmouth, goalpost, goals-against average, goaltender, left-wing pass, left-winger, play off (*v.*), playoff (*n., adj.*), power play, power-play goal, red-line, right-winger, short-handed (*adj.*), shut out (*v.*), shutout (*n., adj.*), slapshot

Hockey Canada (governing body of amateur hockey in Canada)

hodgepodge (*no hyphen*)

Hodgkin's disease

Hogtown (nickname for Toronto)

hold up (*v.*), holdup (*n.*)

H

hole, buttonhole, pigeonhole

Holidays–Capitalize religious holidays and feasts
and all special times: Christmas Eve, Easter,
Hanukkah, Yom Kippur, Ramadan, New
Year's Day, Father's Day.

Hollinger Inc.

Holocaust (murder by Nazis of six million Jews),
holocaust (all other meanings)

Holt, Renfrew and Co. Ltd.
–*but* Holt Renfrew (no comma)

Holy Father (the Pope, *but avoid*)

Holy Land

Holy See (Vatican)

Holy Week

home, homebrew, homebuyer, homegrown,
homemade, homeowner, home page (*two
words*), homesick, hometown, homework

homey (*not* homy)

Hong Kong Special Administrative Region,
People's Republic of China (formal name,
Hong Kong *OK in all references*)

honky-tonk (*hyphen*)

honour, honourable *but* honorary

hoof, hoofs

Hook of Holland

hoopla

Horse Racing–race card, racecourse, racehorse,
racetrack, raceway.

horseback (*one word*)

hospital, hospital commission
–Shaughnessy Hospital
–St. John's General Hospital
–Hospital for Sick Children
–Laval hospital commission

hot, hotbox, hotcake, hotdog, hotfoot, hothead,
hothouse, hotline (show, *prefer* open-line),

H

Hotmail (trademark, *uppercase)*, hotplate, hotrod, hotshot (all one word); *but* hot air, hot-blooded, hot cross bun, hot potato, hot spot, hot water

hotel
–Royal York Hotel
–Fairmont Hotel Vancouver
–a Vancouver hotel

House of Commons (Canadian and British)
–the House, the Commons
–the lower house (Commons)
–House leader Jean Roy (federal)
–the house (provincial)
–house leader Jean Roy (provincial)

hovercraft
–SRN-6 hovercraft
–British Hovercraft Corp.

HSBC Bank Canada
HTML (Hypertext Markup Language)
hubbub
Hudson Bay
Hudson's Bay Co., the Bay
Hudson's Hope, B.C.
Hu Jintao, Hu *(second reference)*
hullabaloo
Hull, Que. – *See Gatineau*
Human Development Resources Canada
humdinger
humdrum *(no hyphen)*
humongous
humour *but* humorous, humorist
Huntington's disease
hurricane Hazel
Hush Puppies (trademark for casual shoes)
Hussein, Saddam, Saddam *(second reference)*
Hutterites

hydroelectric (*no hyphen*)
Hydro-Québec (*hyphen*)
hyperlink
hypocrisy, hypocrite
hypothesis, hypotheses
hysterectomy
Hyundai Auto Canada Inc.
    –Hyundai Corp. (parent company)

Iacocca, Lee
I-beam
ice age (*no single period*)
icebreaker (*no hyphen*)
ice cream, ice-cream bar
icewine (*one word*)
ICU (*OK for* intensive care unit *in second reference*)
ID (identification, *no periods*)
Idaho (*no abbvn.*)
idiosyncrasy
i.e. (*prefer* that is)
IGM Financial Inc. (TSX:IGM)
    –Investors Group Inc.
    –Mackenzie Financial Corp.
Ignatieff, Michael (author)
Ikea (*not* IKEA)
Iles de la Madeleine
ill, ill feeling, ill will; *but* ill-fated, ill-mannered,
    ill-starred
Illecillewaet, B.C.
Illinois (Ill.)
illusion (false impression), allusion (indirect
    reference)
Imax (big-screen movies)
imitator (*not* -er)
immanent (pervading, inherent), imminent
    (impending)
Immigration and Refugee Board
immovable (*not* -eable)
imperial, imperial measure
Imperial Oil Ltd. (TSX:IMO)
impetus, impetuses
implement (*n.* and *v.*), implementation
impostor (*not* -er)
impresario (*not* -ss-)
impressionism (school of art), impressionistic

style

in, inbound, indoor, in-depth, infighting, in-group, in-house, in-law; break-in, cave-in, stand-in, walk-in, write-in

inaccessible (*not* -able)

inadmissible (*not* -able)

inadvertent (*not* -ant)

Inco Ltd. (TSX:N; formerly International Nickel Co.)

income tax

–income tax deduction

incompatibility, incompatible

Incorporated–*Use* Inc. in business names.

incorruptible (*not* -able)

Independence Day (U.S.)

independent, Independent (MP), Ind (*abbvn., no period*)

in depth, in-depth (*adj.*)

index, indexes

Indiana (Ind.)

indict, indictable

indigenous

indispensable (*not* -ible)

Industrial Revolution

Indy-car race

infallible

infantry, 4th Infantry Battalion

infinitesimal

inflammable – *Use* flammable

inflammation, inflammatory

In Flanders Fields (First World War poem by John McCrae)

Infomart

information highway (*lowercase*)

Informetrica

infrared

ING Canada Inc. (TSX:IIC.LV)

ingenious (clever), ingenuous (frank, innocent)
inherent
in-line skating
innocuous
innovate, innovation, innovator
Innu (Aboriginal Peoples in Labrador)
innuendo, innuendoes
inoculate, inoculation
inquire, inquiry, inquiries
  –Cincinnati Enquirer
  –Philadelphia Inquirer
Inquisition, Spanish
inscribe (*not* enscribe), inscription
insignia (*sing.* and *pl.*)
insistence (*not* -ance), insistent (*not* -ant)
inspector, Insp. John Smith
install, installation
instalment
instant message, messaging (IM, *but avoid*)
instil, instilled
institute
  –Women's Institute
insure (cover loss)
intefadeh (Palestinian uprising)
intelligence quotient (IQ)
Interac (banking)
Inter-American Development Bank (IDB, *but avoid)*
Inter American Press Association (IAPA, *but avoid)*
intercollegiate (*no hyphen*)
intercontinental (*no hyphen*)
Intercounty Baseball League
interdependence (*no hyphen*)
interfere, interference
interferon (*lowercase*)
Interior, the (B.C.)
interleague (baseball)

intern (hospital)

International Bank for Reconstruction and
 Development (World Bank)

International Civil Aviation Organization (ICAO)

International Court of Justice (*no abbvn.*)

international date line

International Development Association (IDA, *but
 avoid*)

International Grains Arrangement (*no abbvn.*)

International Joint Commission (IJC, *but avoid*)

International Labour Organization (ILO)

International Monetary Fund (IMF)

International Space Station (ISS, *but avoid*)

International Telecommunications Satellite
 Consortium (Intelsat *OK in first reference)*

International Wheat Agreement, the agreement

Internet–Capitalize specific proper names.
> –Internet, the Net
> –World Wide Web, *but* the web
> –Adobe Acrobat, JavaScript

Lowercase descriptive or generic terms.
> –electronic mail, e-mail
> –blog, chat room, cyberspace, domain name,
> home page, hyperlink, instant messaging,
> shareware
> –web, web browser, webcam, webcast,
> web-enabled, webmaster, web page, weblog,
> web server, website

Use all caps for well-known acronyms and
 abbreviations.
> –CD-ROM, FTP, HTML, HTTP (but
> lowercase in web addresses), RAM, URL

If providing an Internet address, follow upper
 and lowercase of actual address. Include
 www if appropriate: www.cp.org.

If a company uses a variation of its Internet

address as its corporate name, capitalize the
first word: Amazon.com.

interpreter (*not* -or)

interracial (*no hyphen*)

intervene, intervener (*not* -or)

Intracoastal Waterway (*not* Inter-)

intranet (*lowercase*)

Inuit Tapiriit Kanatami (Inuit organization, means
Inuit are united in Canada)

Inuk (*sing. n.* and *adj.*), Inuit (*pl. n.* and *adj.*)

Inukshuk (stone figure)

Inuktitut (language)

inundate, inundation

Inuvialuit (western Arctic aboriginals)

Inuvik, N.W.T.

IODE – *See National Chapter of Canada IODE*

Iowa (*no abbrvn.*)

IPod (*not* iPod)

Ipsco Inc. (TSX:IPS)

Ipsos-Reid (polling company)

Iqaluit, Nunavut

IRA (Irish Republican Army)

iridescent

Irish Republican Army (IRA)

Iron Curtain (outmoded term)

ironic, ironically (*use advisedly*; it does not mean
coincidentally)

irrelevant

irreparable

irresistible (*not* -able)

irreverent (*not* -ant)

island

    –Vancouver Island

    –the Island (informal for Vancouver Island
and P.E.I.)

Ismailia (*not* Ismailiya)

Ispat Sidbec Inc. (Quebec steel company)
IT (for information technology; *spell out*)
Itar-Tass news agency
it's (it is, it has; similar to he's, she's)
    –its (possessive; similar to his, hers)
ITunes (*not* iTunes)
IUD (acceptable on first reference for intra-uterine
    device)
Ivy League

jackhammer
jack pine
Jackson's Point, Ont.
Jacuzzi (trademark for whirlpool tub)
Jaffer, Rahim (politician)
jail (facility, usually provincial, where people are held
    temporarily or serve sentences of two years
    less a day)
    –county jail, jailbird, jailbreak
    –Don Jail (capped when part of formal name)
jalabiya (robe-type garment worn in Africa and the
    Middle East)
Javex (trademark for bleach)
Jaws of Life (trademark for extraction equipment)
Jaycees International, the Jaycees
Jean Coutu Group (TSX:PJC.SV.A)
jeep (for the military vehicle), Jeep (for the
    trademark sport utility vehicle)
Jeff Russel Trophy (football)
Jehovah
Jehovah's Witnesses
    –a Jehovah's Witness, a Witness
Jell-O (trademark for gelatin dessert)
jerry-built
Jet Ski (trademark for personal watercraft)
JetStar
Jew (for man and woman, *not* Jewess)
    –Reform Jew
    –Orthodox Jew
jeweller, jewelry
Jiang Zemin, Jiang (*second reference*)
Jidda, Saudi Arabia
jihad (Arab noun for struggle to do good; often
    used to mean holy war)
jodhpurs
john (lavatory; prostitute's customer)

J

Johns Hopkins Hospital, University
Joint Task Force 2 (Canadian Forces counter-terrorism
        response unit)
joual (Quebec dialect)
Journal de Montréal, Le (newspaper)
Journal de Quebéc, Le (newspaper)
JTI-Macdonald Corp. (formerly RJR-Macdonald Inc.)
Juan Carlos de Borbon
        –Juan Carlos I (king of Spain)
jubilee, Golden Jubilee
judge, Judge Catherine Tracy
judgment (*not* judgement)
Juilliard School of Music
jumbo jet (wide-bodied jet plane, including the Boeing
        747, Lockheed, L-1011, DC-10 and Airbus)
junior
        –John Jones Jr. (*no comma*)
Juno Awards, Junos
jury, grand jury
justice (usually reserved for appeal court judges;
        otherwise, use judge)
        –Chief Justice Albert Weisman, Justice Jean
        Dupont, Justice Sadie Kells (*not* Madam Justice)
        –Smith or the judge or justice in second
        reference
justice of the peace
        –justice of the peace Jean Isaac

K

Kabul, Afghanistan
Kaczynski, Theodore (unabomber)
Kandahar, Afghanistan
kaffeeklatsch
Kahnawake
kaiser, Kaiser Wilhelm
kamikaze
Kampuchea (now Cambodia)
Kaposi's sarcoma (AIDS-related cancer)
Karadzic, Radovan
karaoke
karat (gold), carat (gems)
Karsh, Yousuf (photographer, 1908-2002)
Kathmandu
Kazaa
Kazakhstan
Kejimkujik National Park, N.S.
Kenora Miner and News
Kentucky (Ky.)
kerfuffle
ketchup
keynote (*no hyphen*)
Keystone Kops
KGB (acceptable in all references for the Russian
        words meaning Committee of State Security;
        but include a descriptive phrase such as
        former Soviet secret police)
Khachaturian, Aram (composer, 1903-1978)
Khadafy – *See Gadhafi*
khaki
Khan, Genghis (c. 1162-1227)
Khmer Rouge
Khomeini, Ayatollah Ruhollah (1902-1989)
Khrushchev, Nikita (1894-1971)
kibbutz (communal farm), kibbutzim (*pl.*),
        kibbutznik (resident)

kibitz, kibitzer

kick back (*v.*), kickback (*n.*), kick off (*v.*), kickoff (*n.*)

kidnap, kidnapped, kidnapper

Kiev – *Use* Kyiv

kilo (*avoid* as an abbreviation for kilogram or kilometre)

kilobyte (KB – *sing.* and *pl.* metric symbol)

kilometre (km – *sing.* and *pl.* metric symbol, *no period*) –km/h

Kimberley, B.C.

Kimberly-Clark

kimchee (Korean dish)

kimono, kimonos

kindergarten

King, William Lyon Mackenzie (1874-1950) –usually just Mackenzie King; King *on second reference*

King (of the U.K. and Canada), king (other nations)

Kingston Whig-Standard

Kinsmen Clubs

Kiss (*not* KISS) rock group

Kitchener-Waterloo Record – *Use* Waterloo Region Record

Kish, Nehemiah (ballet)

kitsch

Kitty Litter (trademark for cat litter)

Kiwanis International

Kleenex (trademark for paper tissue)

klieg lights (limelight)

Klondike

Kluane National Park

klutz (a bungler)

Kmart stores (*not* K-Mart)

km/h (kilometres per hour)

Knesset (Israeli parliament)

knick-knack (*hyphen*)

knight
    –Knights of Columbus
    –Knights of Pythias
know-how (*hyphen*)
knowledgeable
Kool-Aid
Kootenai River (U.S.)
Kootenay East, West (B.C. regions)
Kootenay River (B.C.)
Koran – *Use* Qur'an
Kostunica, Vojislav (Yugoslav politician)
Kosygin, Alexei (1904-1980)
Kouchibouguac National Park, N.B.
kowtow
Krakow, Poland
Krazy Glue (trademark for instant glue)
krebiozen (cancer drug)
Kreviazuk, Chantal (singer)
Krieghoff, Cornelius (1815-1872)
krona, kronur (Icelandic currency)
krona, kronor (Swedish currency)
krone, kroner (Danish and Norwegian currency)
Kuerti, Anton (pianist)
Ku Klux Klan
kung fu
Kurelek, William (painter, 1927-1977)
Kuujjuaq, Que.
Kwanlin Dun First Nation (Yukon)
Kyiv (*not* Kiev)
Kyoto Protocol (*but* Kyoto agreement, accord)
Kyrgyzstan (formerly Kirghizia), Kyrgyz (*n., adj.*)

L

La, Le–When lowercase in names, capitalize only at
the start of the sentence. Prefer "the" before
French names of associations and groups;
capitalize "le" or "la" when it is the first word
of the title of a book, song, play and the like.

L.A. (*OK in second reference* for Los Angeles; *use periods*)

Labatt (part of Belgium-based Interbrew)

–Labatt Brewing Co.

–Labatt (*not* Labatt's) announced

–Labatt's beer

label, labelled

labour *but* laborious

Labour Day (*not* Labor Day)

labour sympathizer (union)

Labour sympathizer (party)

–Labour party

Labradorian (resident of Labrador)

Labrador Party

Labrador retriever

Lac de Gras, N.W.T.

Lac La Biche, Alta.

Ladies' Home Journal

Lady Byng Trophy (hockey)

Lake–Capitalize as part of a proper name: Eels Lake,
Lake Huron. Lowercase in plural use: lakes
Erie and Ontario, Eels and Duck lakes.

Lake of the Woods, Ont.

Lake Shore Boulevard (Toronto)

lama (monk), llama (animal)

LaMarsh, Judy (1924-1980)

lambaste, lambaster, lambasting

Lamborghini

landau (horse-drawn carriage)

landmine (*one word*)

Land Rover (trademark)

lang, k.d.

L'Annonciation, Que.
laptop (computer)
largemouth (bass)
largesse
larva, larvae
laryngitis
larynx, larynxes
lasagna
laser (for light amplification by stimulated emission
    of radiation)
Lassa fever
lasso, lassos
L'Assomption, Que.
Last Spike (driven into railway at Craigellachie,
    B.C., on Nov. 7, 1885)
Last Supper
Latin America (*no hyphen*)
laudable
Laumann, Silken (rower)
Laurence, Margaret (author, 1926-1987)
Laurier, Sir Wilfrid (1841-1919)
    –Wilfrid Laurier University
Lavalin Group Inc.
Lavigne, Avril (musician)
law
    –Law of the Sea conference
lawsuit
Lay–This is an action word; it takes a direct object:
    The gunman lays the rifle down, is laying it
    down, laid it down, has laid it down, had laid
    it down, will lay it down.
lay off (*v.*), layoff (*n.*)
lead (*v.*), led, leading
Leader–Capitalize as a semi-official title when used
    with the name of a political party and directly
    preceding a name.

L

    –NDP Leader Jack Layton
    –*but* party leader Jack Layton
    –deputy leader Jean Roy
    –former Tory leader Joe Clark
    –House leader Tony Valeri (federal)
    –house leader Claude Littlefeathers
    (provincial)
    –Japanese leader Junichiro Koizumi
leading seaman (*no abbvn.*)
league
    –League of Nations
    –National Hockey League (NHL)
    –American League (baseball)
    –Catholic Women's League
leap, leapfrog (*n.* and *v.* – *no hyphen*), leap year
Learjet (trademark)
le Carré, John (author)
Led Zeppelin
leery (*not* leary)
leeway
Left Bank (Paris)
left, left field, left-fielder, left wing, left-winger,
    left-field wall, left-handed pitcher, left-wing
    politician (*adj.*, *hyphen*)
left-handed, left-hander (*hyphens*)
legation, Canadian Legation, the legation
Léger, Paul-Émile (1904-1991, former Roman
    Catholic cardinal
legion
    –Foreign Legion
    –Royal Canadian Legion, the legion
legionnaire
legionnaires' disease
Legislature–Capitalize national legislatures;
    lowercase others.
    –Parliament, House of Commons, Commons,

L

House *but* lower house; Senate *but* upper house; Congress, House of Representatives, House; Chamber of Deputies, Chamber; Knesset, Bundestag, French National Assembly.

–Quebec national assembly, Manitoba legislature, Newfoundland and Labrador house of assembly; legislature, house.

legislature member, member of the legislature

leitmotif

le May Doan, Catriona (speed skater)

lend, lent (*v.*), loan (*n.*)

lenience

Lent (season)

Leningrad – *Use* St. Petersburg

Leonardo da Vinci (1452-1519), Leonardo (*not* da Vinci) *on second reference*

Leopard 1 (tank)

Lepreau, Point

leukemia

Levi's (trademark for a brand of jeans)

Lewiston Maineiacs (hockey team)

Lhasa, Tibet

liaison

libel, libelled, libellous

liberal (philosophical attitude)

–a liberal education

Liberal (party or member)

–the Liberal party

–Liberal Party of Canada (formal name)

liberty, liberty boat, *but* Liberty ship

–Statue of Liberty

–the Liberty Bell

library, Toronto Public Library, National Library (capitalize official names)

Libya, Libyan

L

licence (*n.*), license (*v.*)

licensed, licensee, licensing

Lie–This verb, meaning to recline or be situated, does not take a direct object: Trudeau lies in state, is lying in state, lay in state, has lain in state, had lain in state, will lie in state.

lie (*n.*), lie-detector

Liechtenstein

lieutenant (Lieut. *but* Lt.- as prefix in compounds: Lt.-Col.)
    –second lieutenant (2nd Lieut. Anne Finlay)

lieutenant-colonel (Lt.-Col. John Smith)
    –lieutenant-colonels

lieutenant-commander (Lt.-Cmdr. Stan Lyubic)

lieutenant-general (Lt.-Gen. Lee Ward)
    –lieutenant-generals

lieutenant-governor, lieutenant-governors
    –Lt.-Gov. Carole Pelletier
    –the lieutenant-governor said ...

life (*prefix*), lifebelt, lifeboat, lifebuoy, life cycle, lifeguard, life-jacket, lifeless, lifelike, lifeline, lifelong, life-preserver, life-raft, life-size, lifespan, lifestyle, life-support, lifetime, life-work

Life Saver (trademark for a brand of candy)

lightface (type)

light heavyweight

lighthouse, lightkeeper

light-year

likable (*not* -eable)

lime, lime-kiln (*hyphen*), limelight (*no hyphen*)

Limey (slang for British, considered offensive, *avoid*)

Limited–Use Ltd. and ltée (*lowercase, no period)* in business names.

linage (advertising), lineage (ancestry)

linchpin (*not* lynchpin)
Lincoln Center
line, line 2
lineage (ancestry), linage (number of lines)
lineman (football player), linesman (hockey official)
line up (*v.*), lineup (*n.*)
Lions Gate Bridge
Lions, Gulf of
Lion's Head, Ont.
liquefied natural gas (LNG)
liquefy, liquefier, liquefaction
liqueur
lira, lire (*pl.*)
Listuguj (Mi'kmaq band)
Liszt, Franz (1811-1886)
litre (l – *sing.* and *pl.* metric symbol, *no period*)
Little League Baseball World Series
livable (*not* -eable)
living room
LLD (doctor of laws, *but avoid*)
Lloyd Webber, Andrew (composer)
Lloyd's (insurance market, shipping information)
    –Lloyds Bank (no apostrophe)
loan (*n.*), lend, lent (*v.*)
loan shark (*n. only – two words*)
loath (unwilling), loathe (despise)
Loblaw Cos. Ltd. (TSX:L)
    –Loblaw (corporate reference)
    –Loblaws store, Loblaws (retail outlets)
Local 14 (union)
Locations, Places, Sites–Capitalize the names of
    important buildings, residences, historical
    and battle sites, universities and colleges,
    hospitals and hotels. Capitalize Union
    Station, Grand Central Station as important
    buildings but not when known by name of

railway or town: the Via Rail station, Leaside station. Capitalize the names of parks, gardens, playing fields and arenas. Lowercase post offices and courthouses.

locker-room

lock out (*v.*), lockout (*n.*)

lock up (*v.*), lockup (*n.*)

lodge, Orange Lodge
  –the lodge meeting

London Free Press

long distance, a long-distance phone call

long house

Long Island Rail Road

long (*suffix*), daylong, yearlong *but* month-long, week-long

long johns

longliner (fishing vessel)

long-range, a long-range forecast

long-standing, a long-standing rule

long-term (*adj.*)

longtime (*no hyphen*, compound modifier)

Longueuil, Que.

loonie (dollar coin), loony (insane), Looney Tunes (cartoons)

loophole (*no hyphen*)

looseleaf (*no hyphen*)

loran (for long-range air navigation system)

Lords, the (institution), lords (members), Lord's (cricket ground)

Lord's Prayer, the

Lord Thomson of Fleet (*but avoid*)

L'Orignal, Ont.

Losier-Cool, Rose-Marie (senator)

Loto-Québec (*hyphen*)

Lotto 6-49

Louisbourg, N.S.

–Fortress of Louisbourg
Louisiana (La.)
Lou Marsh Trophy
lovable (*not* -eable)
lowbrow (*no hyphen*)
Lower Canada (name for southern portion of
     Québec from 1791 to 1840)
lowercase (*n., v.*)
lower house
Lower Mainland (B.C.)
Lower Manhattan (New York City)
Lower Town (Quebec or Ottawa)
LSD (acceptable in all references for lysergic acid
     diethylamide)
Luftwaffe
Lunenburg, N.S.
Lutz (figure-skating jump)
Luxembourg
luxury, luxurious
Lycra (trademark for spandex fibre)
Lyme disease

M

MA (master of arts)
    –a master's degree
Macau
Macdonald, Angus L. (Nova Scotia politician,
    1890-1954; Halifax bridge)
MacDonald, Ann-Marie (writer)
Macdonald-Cartier Freeway, Highway 401
Macdonald College
MacDonald, Flora
MacDonald, J.E.H. (painter, 1873-1932)
Macdonald, Sir John A. (1815-1891)
Macdonald, Man.
mace (staff of office; club), mace-bearer
Mace (trademark for a paralysing spray)
MacEachen, Allan (politician)
MacGregor, Man.
Mach (speed, after physicist Ernest Mach)
machiavellian
machine-gun
    –submachine-gun
Macintosh (computer)
    –*but* McIntosh (apple)
MacIsaac, Ashley
MacKay, Peter (politician)
Mackenzie, Alexander (1822-1892)
Mackenzie Financial Corp. – *See IGM Financial Inc.*
Mackenzie Highway, River, Valley
MacKenzie, Lewis
Mackenzie, William Lyon (patriot, 1795-1861;
    grandfather of William Lyon Mackenzie
    King)
mackinaw (cloth, heavy coat)
mackintosh (coat)
Mack Truck (trademark)
MacLean, Ron (sportscaster)
Maclean's magazine

MacLennan, Hugh (author, 1907-1990)
Macmillan Canada (former publisher)
MacMillan, Sir Ernest (1893-1973)
MacNeil, Rita (singer)
Macphail, Agnes (Canada's first woman MP, 1890-1954)
Macpherson, Kay (feminist, 1913-1999)
madam (polite form of address; brothel-keeper)
madame (French title of respect)
    –Madame Robert Duval (*no abbvn.*)
mad cow disease (*OK in first reference* for BSE)
mademoiselle (*no abbvn.*)
Madonna (performer), the Madonna (mother of Jesus)
maelstrom
Mafia; Mafioso, Mafiosi (member, *sing.* and *pl.*)
Magazine–Capitalize when part of the actual title.
    –New York Times Magazine
    –Maclean's magazine
    Time magazine
Magdalen Islands (*prefer* Iles de la Madeleine)
Magna Carta (*not* Charta)
Magna International Inc. (TSX:MG.SV.A)
Magnum (trademark for a cartridge), a .357-calibre Magnum revolver, a Colt Python .357
Magnum
mail-order catalogue (*hyphen*)
Maine (*no abbvn.*)
mainframe
major (Maj. Alice Lajoie)
major-general (Maj.-Gen. Keith Adams), major-generals
make up (*v.*), makeup (*n.*), makeover (*n.*)
malemute (dog)
Mallorca
Mamma Mia (musical, *not* Mamma Mia!)

M

mammogram, mammography (breast X-ray)
mandarin (civil servant); Mandarin (Chinese
    dialect)
manhattan (cocktail)
manhunt
manila paper
Manila, Philippines
Manitoba (Man.)
Manitoba Telecom Services Inc. (TSX:MBT)
manoeuvre
Man of the Year
man-of-war (warship)
    –Man o' War (racehorse)
mantel (fireplace)
mantle (cloak)
Manulife Financial Corp. (TSX:MFC)
Mao Zedong, Mao (*second reference*)
    –Maoism
maple leaf, leaves
    –Maple Leaf (flag, emblem)
    –Toronto Maple Leafs
Maple Leaf Foods Inc. (TSX:MFI)
Maple Leaf Gardens
March (*no abbvn.*)
march past (*n.* and *v.*)
Mardi Gras
marijuana
marine, marine corps
    –U.S. Marine Corps
    –Royal Marines
    –a marine, the marines, marine offensive, etc.
maritime
    –Maritime provinces, the Maritimes
    –New Brunswick, Nova Scotia, P.E.I.
    –The Atlantic provinces comprise the
    Maritimes and Newfoundland and Labrador.

Maritime Employers Association (MEA, *but avoid*)
Mark III, Mark 46 (follow maker's style)
marketplace
Mark, Inky (politician)
Marks & Spencer
Marleau, Diane (politician)
marquess *but* Marquis of Queensberry rules
Marquis wheat
Marrakech (*not* Marrakesh)
Marseille
marshal (*n.* and *v.*), marshalled, fire marshal,
      parade marshal
Marshall Plan
martini
Martyrs' Shrine (at Midland, Ont.)
marvellous
Marxism, Marxist
Maryland (Md.)
Mase (rap singer)
MASH
mason (person who builds with stone)
Mason (member of Masonic order)
Masonite (a trademark for a brand of hardboard)
Mason jar
mass, low mass, high mass, requiem mass
Massachusetts (Mass.)
massasauga (rattlesnake)
mastectomy
MasterCard
master corporal (Master Cpl. Pierre Charest)
masterful (domineering), masterly (skilful)
master of arts (MA), a master's degree
master of ceremonies (MC)
Masters, the (golf tournament)
master seaman (*no abbvn.*)
master sergeant (Master Sgt.)

M

master warrant officer (*no abbvn.*)

matchup (*n.*), match up (*v.*)

matrix, matrixes

matzo, matzos

maximum, maximums

mayday (distress signal)

mayonnaise

mayor, Mayor Grace McDonald
>   –the mayor of Ottawa
>   –former mayor Ken Elman
>   –acting mayor Ken Elman
>   –the acting mayor
>   –mayor-elect Ken Elman
>   –Deputy Mayor Patrick Keenan (formal title)

mayoralty (*n.*), mayoral (*adj.*)

mazel tov (good luck)

MC (master of ceremonies), MCs, MCing, MCed,
>   *but use only* when meaning is clear from context

McCarthy, Joseph (U.S. senator, 1945-1957)

McCarthy Tétrault (legal firm)

McClelland & Stewart Ltd. (publisher)

McClung, Nellie (feminist, 1873-1951)

M'Clure Strait (in Arctic); named after explorer Sir
>   Robert M'Clure (1807-73)

McCrae, John (1872-1918, poet who wrote In
>   Flanders Fields)

McDonald's Restaurants of Canada Ltd.
>   –McDonald's

McDonnell Douglas Canada Ltd.

McDonough, Alexa (politician)

McEntire, Reba (singer)

McGraw-Hill Ryerson Ltd. (publisher)

McIntosh apple
>   –*but* Macintosh (computer)

McLachlan, Sarah (singer)

McLachlin, Beverley (Supreme Court chief justice)

McLaren, Norman (filmmaker, 1914-1987)
McLauchlan, Murray (folksinger)
McLaughlin, Audrey (former NDP leader)
McLellan, Anne (politician)
McLuhan, Marshall (1911-1980)
McPherson, Aimee Semple (evangelist, 1890-
      1944)
MDS Inc. (TSX:MDS)
meagre (*not* -ger)
Meals on Wheels
meat packer (*two words*) *but* meat-packing
Mecca (place)
      –*but* a music mecca
medal, medallist
Medals–Capitalize specific names.
      –Medal of Bravery
      –the Military Medal (MM)
      –a military medal
medevac
Medicaid (U.S. program of health care for poor)
medicare (government medical insurance plan in
      general), Medicare (U.S. health program)
medieval
Mediterranean
medium, media (*pl.* – except mediums in
      spiritualism)
Meech Lake accord
meerschaum (pipe)
Mehta, Deepa (filmmaker)
member
      –member of Parliament (MP, MPs)
      –member of the Order of the British Empire
      (MBE)
      –member of provincial parliament
      (MPP – Ontario only, *but avoid*)

–member of house of assembly
(MHA – N.L. only, *but avoid*)
–member of legislative assembly
(MLA, *but avoid*)
–member of national assembly
(MNA – Quebec only, *but avoid*)
memento, mementoes
memo, memos
memoir (*not* memoire)
    –*but* aide-mémoire
memorandum, memorandums
Mendelssohn, Felix (composer, 1809-1847)
meningitis, meningococcal disease
Mennonite
menswear, womenswear
MenTV (specialty channel)
Mercator projection
Mercedes-Benz
merchant marine
Messiah, a messiah
Messrs. – *Use* Messieurs (before names)
meter (gauge)
methadone
Métis (mixed Indian and European ancestry)
metre (m – *sing.* and *pl.* metric symbol, *no period);*
    but diameter
metrication (*not* metrification)
Metro Inc. (TSX:MRU.SV.A)
Mexico City
MHA (N.L. only – member of house of assembly,
    but avoid)
MI-5, MI-6 (British intelligence)
Michigan (Mich.)
mickey (half-sized bottle of liquor)
Micmac – *Use* Mi'kmaq
micro (*prefix*), microsurgery, microwave,

micro-organism
microphone, mike
midday
Middle Ages
Middle (*not* Near) East
Middle West, Midwest (U.S.)
Mideast
midshipman (*no abbvn.*)
midsummer (*no hyphen*)
midway (*no hyphen*)
MiG (for Russian aircraft designers Mikoyan and Gurevich)
Mi'kmaq (*not* Micmac)
mileage (*not* milage; for metric, *use* consumption or fuel consumption)
Military Rank–Plurals add "s" to the significant rank category, not to the qualifying word.
  –major-generals
  –lieutenant-colonels
  –sergeants major
  –regimental sergeants major
millennium (-nn-), millenniums
Miller, Glenn (band leader, 1904-1944)
Millett, Kate (writer)
millimetre (mm – *sing.* and *pl.* metric symbol, *no period*)
Milosevic, Slobodan (former Serbian leader)
Milquetoast, Caspar
Minamata, Japan
  –Minamata disease
Mini–Hyphenate unless the non-hyphenated form is established.
  –mini-budget, mini-play, mini-restaurant, mini-sub, but minibike, minibus, minicar, miniseries, miniskirt, minivan
minimum, minimums

minister
   –Energy Minister Joe Carney; Joe Carney, energy
   minister

Ministry–Capitalize national and provincial
   government ministries when a shorter
   version of the full name is used.
   –Ministry of the Interior, Interior Ministry
   –Ministry of Transportation and
   Communications, Communications Ministry
   –The freeze affected Industry and Labour.
   Do not capitalize when shorter version is used
   as an adjective.
   –health spokesman
   – *See Department*

Minnesota (Minn.)

mint, Royal Canadian Mint, the mint

minus, minuses

minuscule (*not* miniscule)

Minute Rice (trademark for quick-cooking rice)

minutia, minutiae

Miramichi River (N.B.), the Miramichi area

MIRV (for multiple independently targeted
   re-entry vehicle; always needs explanation)

misinterpret, misinterpreter, misinterpretation

mislead, misled, misleading

Mississauga, Ont.

Mississauga IceDogs

Mississippi (Miss.)

Missouri (Mo.)

Mitchell, Joni (singer)

Mixmaster (trademark for food mixer)

MLA (except Ont., Que. and N.L. – member of the
   legislative assembly) *but avoid*

Mladic, Ratko (Bosnian Serb general)

MNA (Que. – member of national assembly) *but
   avoid*

M

Mob (for Mafia), mob (other uses)
moccasin
Mogadishu
Mohammed – *See Muhammad*
Mohawk (*sing.* and *pl.*)
Moldova (formerly Moldavia)
mollusk
Molotov cocktail
Molson Coors Brewing Co. (TSX:TAP.NV)
   –Molson Coors Canada Inc. (Canadian
   division)
Moncton Times and Transcript
money, moneys
money laundering (no hyphen)
monitor
monkey, monkeys
Monroe, Marilyn (1926-1962)
monsieur (*no abbvn.*), messieurs
monsignor, Msgr. Ronald Thom
   –Thom (or the monsignor) said ...
Montana (Mont.)
Monterey, Calif.
Monterrey (Spain, Mexico)
Montgomery, Lucy Maud (1874-1942)
Months–In dates, abbreviate except March, April,
   May, June, July: Jan. 13, 1936; April 2, 1981,
   was a Thursday; *but* January 2005, *no commas.*
month-long
moon
Moose Jaw Times-Herald
moral (*n.* – lesson, inner meaning; *adj.* – right, just),
   moralist, morality
morale (*n.* – mental condition, attitude)
Moral Majority (*no* "the")
Morgentaler, Dr. Henry
Morissette, Alanis (musician)

M

Moriyama, Raymond (architect)

morocco leather

Mormons (*acceptable in first reference* for Church of Jesus Christ of Latter-day Saints)

Morrice, J.W. (painter, 1865-1924)

Morse code

Moslem – *Use* Muslim

mosquito, mosquitoes

Mother's Day (second Sunday in May)

Mother Teresa (1910-1997)

motocross

motto, mottoes

mould (*not* mold)

Mountain–Capitalize when preceding or following specific term.
   –Rocky Mountains
   –Mount Edith Cavell (*not* Mt.)

Mountie, Mounties (for RCMP)

Mount Vesuvius

mouse, mousey, mousier

moustache (*not* mus-)

movable (*not* moveable)

Mowat, Farley (author)

MP (member of Parliament), MPs (*pl.*), MP's and MPs' (*poss.*)

m.p.h. (miles per hour)

MPP (Ontario only – member of the provincial parliament) *but avoid*

MP3.com (company)

MP3 player

MRI (for magnetic resonance imaging; *OK in first reference*)

Ms. (*period*)

MuchMusic, MuchMoreMusic, MuchMoreRetro

mucous (*adj.* – covered with mucus), mucus (*n.* – sticky secretion)

M

Muhammad (for founder of Islam and all other uses   unless user prefers another spelling)

Muhammad Ali

mujahedeen (holy warriors, *pl.*), mujahed (*sing.*)

mukluk (deerskin boot)

mulatto – *Avoid.* Use black-white parentage or some other description.

multi-, multicultural, multilateral, multinational, multimillionaire, multimillion-dollar, multimedia *but* multi-year

Mumbai (formerly Bombay)
   –MUMBAI, India (placeline)

mumps (*takes singular verb*)

Murray, Anne (singer)

Muscovite (of Moscow)

muskellunge, muskie

Muslim (*not* Moslem)

Muzak (trademark for recorded background music)

MV (motor vessel)

Myanmar (formerly Burma, *n.* and *adj.* Burma can be used in historical references.

N

NAACP (National Association for the
     Advancement of Colored People)
NADbank (Newspaper Audience Databank)
naive, naiveté
Namibia (formerly South-West Africa)
Nanaimo Free Press
naphtha
napoleon (French gold coin, pastry)
Nasdaq
Naskapi, Naskapis
nation, *but uppercase* as part of aboriginal name:
     Nisga'a Nation
National, The (CBC news program)
National Action Committee on the Status of
     Women (NAC)
National Aeronautics and Space Administration
     (NASA *OK in first reference*)
national anthem (O Canada)
National Assembly (national legislative body;
     Cuban National Assembly) *but*
     Quebec national assembly (provincial)
National Capital Region
National Chapter Canada IODE (official name of
     Imperial Order of Daughters of the Empire in
     Canada)
National Citizens Coalition *(no apostrophe)*
National Defence Headquarters (NDHQ, *but avoid*)
National Energy Board (NEB, *but avoid*)
national energy program
National Farmers Union (NFU, *but avoid*)
National Film Board (NFB)
National Gallery
national government
National Guard (in U.S.)
     –a National Guard unit
     –a national guardsman
National Hockey League Players' Association

National Library
National Organization for Women (NOW)
National Post, the National Post
National War Memorial (Ottawa)
nationwide (*no hyphen, but prefer* countrywide)
native peoples (includes Indians, Inuit and Métis)
NATO (North Atlantic Treaty Organization)
Natuashish (Labrador community relocated from
    Davis Inlet)
nautical mile (1.853 kilometres)
Nav Canada
Navy–Capitalize Royal Canadian Navy when
    referring to pre-unification force. For other
    forces, lowercase navy when preceded by the
    name of the country.
    –Royal Canadian Navy until 1968
    –British navy
    –Royal Navy
    –U. S. navy
    –a navy spokesman
    –U.S. 6th Fleet
    –Home Fleet
    –10th Destroyer Flotilla
Nazi (party supporter)
Nazism
NBC (National Broadcasting Co.)
    –NBC *acceptable in all references*
N'djamena (Chad)
Nebraska (Neb.)
Negro, Negroes – *Use* black
neighbour, neighbourhood
Neilson Ltd., William (confectioner)
neoclassical, neoclassicalism
Neo-Confucianism
nerve-racking
Netanyahu, Benjamin

N

Netherlands, the
  –UTRECHT, Netherlands (placeline)
Neurochem Inc. (TSX:NRM)
Nevada (Nev.)
New Age (spiritual movement)
New Brunswick (N.B.)
New Brunswick Telegraph Journal
new Canadian
New China news agency (Xinhua)
New Democratic Party (NDP)
New England
newfangled (*one word*)
Newfoundland and Labrador (official name of
    province)
  –N.L. (*abbvn.*)
New Hampshire (N.H.)
New Jersey (N.J.)
newlyweds
New Mexico (N.M.)
news, newsdesk, newsprint, newsroom,
    newsstand, newswire
Newsmaker of the Year (CP)
Newsnet (CTV)
Newspaper Guild, the; the guild
Newspaper Names–Lowercase *the* in names of
    newspapers: the Toronto Star; the Star; the
    New York Times, the Times. For French-
    language papers, write Montreal La Presse
    rather than the Montreal La Presse in first
    reference. In subsequent references avoid
    sentence constructions that juxtapose *the* and
    le and *la*:: the La Presse editorial. Alternatives
    include La Presse said in an editorial, an
    editorial in La Presse.
Newsworld (CBC)
New Testament

New Westminster, B.C.
New World
New Year's Eve, New Year's Day *but* the new year
      (*lowercase*)
New York (N.Y.)
      –New York City
      –New York Thruway
      –New York state
Nexen Inc. (TSX:NXY)
Niagara Escarpment, Peninsula
Niagara-on-the-Lake, Ont.
Nichol, bp (poet, 1944-1988)
nickel (coin or metal)
Nickelback (performing group)
Nicknames–Capitalize nicknames generally.
      –the Old Man
      –Reds (for Communists)
      –the Queen City (Regina)
      –the City (London financial area)
      –Iron Curtain
      –Mike (Pinball) Clemons (brackets, not
      quotes); *but* Pinball Clemons (no brackets)
niece
Nielsen Media Research (TV ratings company)
night, guest night, ladies night
nightcap, nightclub, nightdress, nightgown,
      nighthawk, nightlight, nightmare, night owl,
      night school, nightshirt, nighttime, night
      watch
Nike
Nikon (camera)
Nineteen Eighty-Four (George Orwell novel *but*
      1984 for Michael Radford movie)
Nisga'a, Nisga'a Nation
nitroglycerine
N.L. (abbreviation for Newfoundland and

Labrador)
–ST. JOHN'S, N.L., HAPPY VALLEY-GOOSE
BAY, N.L. (placelines)
no, noes, no-noes
–*but* She voted No in the referendum.
Nobel Prize, Nobel Prizes
–Nobel Peace Prize
–Nobel Prize in chemistry, physics, etc. but
Nobel chemistry prize
–Nobel Memorial Prize in Economic Science
–Nobel Prize winner, laureate
–Nobel Prize-winning researcher
–the prize (*lowercase*)
no man's land
nom de plume, noms de plume
noncommittal
nondescript
non-existent (*not* -ant)
non-fiction (*adj, n.*)
nonplus (*v.*), nonplussed
non-stick (*adj.*)
no one (*two words*)
Norad (North American Aerospace Defence
Command)
Nortel Networks Corp. (TSX:NT)
North–Capitalize geographic regions but not their
derivatives. Lowercase mere direction or
position.
–the North (region of Canada)
–the north (of a province), northern Ontario,
northern Quebec, etc.
–a northerner
–the northern territories
–northern natives
–Northern Canada
–the Canadian North

–the Far North
–the North Slope (Alaska)
–north of the border
–North-South dialogue
–the northern delegation
–the northern states
–The North defeated the South.
–North Atlantic
–Northern Ireland
North American Aerospace Defence Command
    (Norad *OK in first reference*)
North American Free Trade Agreement (NAFTA)
North Atlantic Treaty Organization (NATO *OK in
    first reference*)
North Carolina (N.C.)
North Dakota (N.D.)
northeast, northwest (*one word)*
Northern Hemisphere
northern lights
northern Ontario
northern states (of U.S.)
North Pole, the Pole
North Sea
Northwest Atlantic Fisheries Organization (*no
    abbvn.*)
North West Company
North West Mounted Police
Northwest Passage
Northwest Rebellion (1885)
Northwest Territories (*but* N.W.T.)
    –Northwest Territories council
nose, nosy, nosier
nostalgia, nostalgic
noticeable
Notre-Dame Basilica (Montreal)
Nouvelles Télé-Radio (NTR, the French-language

N

service of Broadcast News)
Nouvelliste, Le (newspaper in Trois Rivières, Que.)
Nova Chemicals Corp. (*not* NOVA; TSX:NCX)
Nova Scotia (N.S.)
Nova Scotia Power Inc. (*no abbvn.*)
Novocain (trademark for a local anesthetic)
NOW (National Organization for Women)
'N Sync (musical group)
NTR (Nouvelles Télé-Radio)
nucleus, nuclei
number, number 2, No. 2
numskull (*not* numbskull)
Nunassiaq, N.W.T.
Nunatsiavut (region of Labrador controlled by
      Inuit)
Nunavut (Canadian territory, *no abbvn.*)
      –Nunavummiut (resident of Nunavut)
Nuremberg, Germany
Nureyev, Rudolf (ballet, 1938-1993)
nylon

O

Oakland Athletics, Oakland A's
O&Y Properties Corp. (*no periods, no spaces* in O&Y)
oasis, oases
Oath of Allegiance (Canada's official oath)
obbligato
Oberammergau
Obhrai, Deepak (politician)
objet d'art, objets d'art
O Canada
Occidental (race; *avoid)*
occur, occurred, occurrence, occurring
Ocean–Capitalize with specific name.
    –Pacific Ocean
    –the Atlantic and Pacific oceans
    –an ocean wave
October Crisis (1970)
octopus, octopuses
Odd Fellows, Independent Order of (IOOF,
    but avoid), an Odd Fellow
Odesa, Ukraine (*not* Odessa)
odour, odourless *but* odorous
OECD (Organization for Economic Co-operation
    and Development)
Oedipus
off, offbeat, off-centre, off-duty, off-line, off-season,
    offshore, offside, offstage, off-white; blastoff
    (*n.*), blast off (*v.*).
   Similarly: cutoff, layoff, payoff, playoff, sendoff,
    standoff, stopoff, takeoff (all *n.*)
offence, offensive
office, county clerk's office
    –Home Office (U.K.)
    –Foreign Office (U.K.)
officer cadet (*no abbvn.*)
    –Officer Cadet Andrew Glenny
officer of the Order of the British Empire (OBE)

O

officers mess
Ohio (*no abbvn.*)
oilfield, oilpatch, oilsands (*one word*)
Ojibwa (Indian – rhymes with way) (*sing.* and *pl.*)
OK (*not* okay), OK'd, OK'ing
OK (*not* OK!) magazine
Okalik, Paul (premier of Nunavut)
Oklahoma (Okla.)
Oklahoma (*not* Oklahoma!) musical
Oktoberfest (beer-drinking festival)
old age pension
Old Boys club, network
old-fashioned
Old Testament
old-time, old-timer
Olivier, Laurence (1907-1989)
Olympic Games, the Games
    –the Winter Olympics, the Olympics, the
    Summer Games
ombudsman, ombudsmen
    –ombudsman Jill Leonard
omelette
Onassis, Aristotle (1906-1975)
Ondaatje, Michael
One-Eleven (British aircraft)
one-time (*adj., hyphen for all uses*)
Onex Corp. (TSX:OCX.SV)
online (all uses)
onstage, offstage
Ontario (Ont.), Ontarian
Ontario Health Insurance Plan (OHIP, *but avoid*)
Ontario Power Generation (formerly Ontario
    Hydro)
Ontario Provincial Police (*but* the provincial police)
onto

O

OPEC (Organization of Petroleum Exporting
    Countries)
ophthalmologist, ophthalmology
Opposition–Capitalize when referring to the
    official Opposition. Otherwise, lowercase.
    –an opposition viewpoint, sat in opposition
    –the Opposition leader
opus, opuses
Orange Crush (trademark for pop)
orbit (*n.* and *v.*), orbital, orbiting
Order of Canada
    –companion of the Order of Canada
    (recipients may use initials CC)
    –officer of the order (initials OC)
    –member of the order (initials CM)
order-in-council, orders-in-council
ordinary seaman (*no abbvn.*)
    –Ordinary Seaman Alain Delisle
Oregon (Ore.)
Organization for Economic Co-operation and
    Development (OECD)
Organization for Security and Co-operation in
    Europe
Organization of African Unity (OAU)
Organization of American States (OAS)
Organization of Petroleum Exporting Countries
    (OPEC)
organize
Orient, Oriental (race; *but use* Asia, Asian)
    –an oriental flavour
    –Orient Express (train)
Orillia Packet and Times
orneriness, ornery
ornithology
orthopedic
Osbourne, Ozzy

O

Osgoode Hall (home of Ontario Appeal Court)
Otello (Verdi and Rossini operas), Othello
    (Shakespeare play)
Ottawa Renegades (CFL team)
Ottawa Rough Riders (former CFL team)
Ottawa 67's (hockey team)
Ouellet, André
out, outbid, outboard, outbox, outfield, outpatient,
    outtake (film); fadeout (*n.*), fade out (*v.*).
    Similarly: fallout, hideout, pullout, shootout,
    shutout, takeout, walkout (all *n.*)
Outaouais, western Quebec
OUTtv
Oval Office
overall, overalls (garment)
overall (all-embracing)
Owen Sound Sun Times
Oxfam Canada
oxford (cloth, shoe)
Ozawa, Seiji (conductor)
ozone

Pablum (trademark for a baby cereal), *but* pabulum (food)

pact, Baghdad Pact, Warsaw Pact

page 2, pages 1-3; p. 2, pp. 1-3 (*abbvn.* for tabulation)

Pahlavi, Mohammad Reza (shah, 1919-1980)

paleontologist, paleontology

Palestine Liberation Organization (PLO)

pallbearer (*one word*)

Palm Pilot

panacea

Panama Canal

panama hat

Panama, Isthmus of

Pan American Games, Pan Am Games (*no hyphen*)

panda (*not* panda bear)

panel, panellist, panelling

pantyhose

paparazzo, paparazzi

paper-boy, paper-clip, paper-girl

Pap smear, test

Papua New Guinea (*no hyphen*)

paraffin (wax; in Britain, kerosene)

paragraph 2

parallel, paralleled, 49th parallel

paralyze (*not* -se), paralysis

paranoia, paranoiac, paranoid

paraphernalia (*pl.*)

paraplegic

parenthesis, parentheses

parimutuel (*no hyphen*)

Parisien Libéré (newspaper – *not* Libre)

park, Banff National Park, High Park

Parker Bowles, Camilla (*now* Duchess of Cornwall)

Parkinson's disease, Parkinsonism

P

Parks Canada
parliament
- –Parliament (national legislature)
- –parliament (provincial or regional)
- –parliamentary
- –Parliament Buildings (Ottawa)
- –Israel's parliament, the Knesset

Parliament, member of (MP, MPs)
parlour
Parmesan cheese
parole, paroled, parolee
Parti indépendantiste
Parti Québécois (PQ), Québécois's (*poss.*)
- –Péquiste (*n., adj.*)

partisan
part time, a part-time job, a part-timer
party, Communist party, Green party, Liberal party
- –*but* New Democratic Party (NDP)
- –Parti Québécois (PQ)

Pashto (language in Afghanistan and Pakistan)
Pashtun (ethnic group in Afghanistan and Pakistan)
Passchendaele
passerby, passersby
pasteurize, pasteurizing
pastime
patchwork (*one word*)
Patriot (U.S. missile)
pavilion (*not* pavillion)
Pavarotti, Luciano
paycheque (*one word*)
payday (*one word*)
pay off (*v.*), payoff (*n.*)
payola
payroll (*no hyphen*)
pay TV, pay TV network (*no hyphen*)
PC (*OK in first reference* for personal computer)

PCB (polychlorinated biphenyl), PCBs
PDA (personal digital assistant)
pea, peameal bacon, pea soup, pea-soup fog,
    pea-souper (fog)
Peace Corps (U.S.)
peacekeeping
peacemaker
peacetime
peak (mountain, apex); peek (peer)
peccadillo, peccadillos
pedagogy
pedal (bicycle), pedaller, pedalling
peddle (to sell), pedlar (seller), peddling, softpedal
    (*not* -peddle)
pediatrician
pedlar (seller)
pedophile
peewee
Peggy's Cove, N.S.
pekinese (dog)
pemmican (dried meat)
Penetanguishene, Ont.
penicillin
penitentiary, Kingston Penitentiary
Pennsylvania (Pa.)
pension, Canada Pension Plan (CPP, *but avoid*)
Pepsi, Pepsi-Cola (trademarks for a cola drink)
pep talk (*two words*)
Péquiste
perceive, perceived, perceiving
per cent, percentage, six per cent increase (*no
    hyphens*)
perennial
perestroika
perfunctory
periphery

P

permafrost (*no hyphen*)
permissible (*not* -able)
perogy, perogies
perquisite (perk), prerequisite (requirement)
Perrier (trademark for a mineral water)
perseverance, persevere, persevering
Pershing, Pershing 2 missile
Persian Gulf War
persian lamb
persistence (*not* -ance), persistency, persistent (*not* -ant)
persona non grata
persuade, persuadable, persuasible, persuasion, persuasive
Petro-Canada (*hyphen; no abbvn.; TSX:PCA*)
petrochemical (*no hyphen*)
petty officer (*no abbvn.*)
    –chief petty officer (first class) (*no abbvn.*)
    –petty officer (first class) (*no abbvn.*)
PGA (Professional Golfers Association)
Phalange party (Lebanon)
pharaoh
phase, Phase 1 (*not* phase one)
PhD (doctor of philosophy)
phenomenon, phenomena
Philadelphia Inquirer (newspaper)
Philadelphia 76ers (*no apostrophe*)
Philip (usual spelling of first name)
    –Prince Philip
Philippe
Philippines, the
    –QUEZON CITY, Philippines (placeline)
    –Filipinos (the people)
philistine (lowercase for someone lacking culture)
Phnom Penh, Cambodia
Phoebe

phoney (*not* phony), phoneys
phosphorus (*not* -ous)
photo-engraver, photo-engraving
phys-ed
piastre (*not* -er)
Picchio Pharma Inc.
piccolo, piccolos
picket (*not* picketer), picketed, picketing
pick up (*v.*), pickup (*n.* or *adj.*)
picnic, picnicker
piecemeal
pigeonhole (*no hyphen*)
pileup (*n.*)
pill (*lowercase* for birth control pill, the pill)
pilot officer (*no abbvn.*)
PIN (personal identification number)
pinch-hitter
Pinot Noir, Blanc (wine)
pin up (*v.*), pin-up (*n.*)
pipeline
      –*but* TransCanada PipeLines Ltd.
pizzazz
placeline
      –CORNER BROOK, N.L.
      –MacGREGOR, Man. (for MacGregor)
      –MACKENZIE, B.C. (for Mackenzie)
Placer Dome Inc. (TSX:PDG)
Places–*See Locations*
plagiarism, plagiarize
plainclothes police
      –police in plain clothes
plan, Colombo Plan, Marshall Plan
plaster of paris
plateau, plateaus
platoon sergeant (Platoon Sgt.)
platypus, platypuses

P

play off (*v.*), playoff (*n.*)
playwright, *but* playwriting
PLC (public limited company)
pleaded (*preferred to* pled for past tense of plead)
Plexiglas (trademark for an acrylic plastic)
PLO (Palestine Liberation Organization)
plow (*not* plough)
plummet, plummeted
plus, pluses
p.m., a.m.
pogey (slang for employment insurance)
poinsettia
Point Lepreau
Polanyi, John (Nobel Prize in chemistry, 1986)
Polaroid (trademark for camera, sunglasses)
Pole, the; North Pole, South Pole
Police–Uppercase when using the formal name of
    a force. Otherwise, lowercase.
      –provincial police, regional police
      –Toronto Police Service, *but* a Toronto police
      officer, Toronto police
      –Ontario Provincial Police (OPP)
      –*but* Quebec provincial police (*no abbvn.*)
      –Royal Canadian Mounted Police (RCMP)
      –Mounties (for RCMP)
      –police chief
      –police Chief Arnold Goldberg, Deputy Chief
      Emma Vokey
      –police commission
      –Quebec police commission
      –police court, station
policy-maker
polio (short for poliomyelitis)
Politburo
Politics–Capitalize political parties, as Liberal,
    Labour, Socialist, *but* lowercase the words

when referring to philosophical attitudes. Capitalize Opposition when referring to the official Opposition, the non-governing party with the most seats.

polka-dot (*hyphen*)

Pollyanna

Ponteix, Sask.

pontiff (for Pope)

pope, Pope Benedict, the Pope (current pontiff), former pope, popes of history

Popsicle (trademark for ice on a stick)

pore (*v.* – study earnestly), pored, poring

Porsche

Portage la Prairie, Man.

Port aux Basques, N.L.

porterhouse steak

portland cement

Portuguese

postdate (*v.*), postdated cheque

postelection

post-game

postgraduate

Post-it notes (trademark)

postmaster general, postmasters general

post-mortem (*hyphen*)

post-season (*hyphen*)

post-secondary

postwar

potato, potatoes

potlatch (aboriginal gift, ceremony)

potshot

poutine

PoW (prisoner of war), PoWs

Power Corp.

power of attorney (*no hyphens*)

powwow (*n.* and *v.*)

P

PR (for public relations)

practicable (can be done), practical (useful, functional)

practice (*n.* or *adj.*), practise (*v.*)

prairie
—Prairie provinces
—the Prairies
—their Prairie farm
—the prairie was parched in drought

pre, prearrange, Precambrian shield, pre-Christian, precondition, predate, pre-election, pre-empt, preheat, premarital, preoccupy, prepaid, preschool, preschooler, pre-season, pre-tax, prewar

precede, precedence (priority)

precedent (earlier instance)

prefer, preferable, preferably, preference (*not* -ance), preferential, preferred

Premier—Use for Canadian provinces, Australian states, France and former French colonies.
—Premier Ann Bostwick
—deputy premier Henry Miller (informal position)
—premiers conference
—former premier Roy Romanow
—the premier of Ontario

première (*n.* and *v.*)
—*but* a premier attraction

prerequisite (requirement), perquisite (perk)

prerogative (*not* perog-)

Presbyterian Church in Canada

president, President George W. Bush
—the president said ...
—former president Bill Clinton
—president-elect Ronald Reagan
—GM president Janice Brown

Presque Isle, Me.
Presqu'ile Point, Ont.
press gallery
 –Parliamentary Press Gallery Association
 –press gallery dinner
 –worked in the press gallery
Presse, La (Montreal newspaper)
Presse Canadienne, La (PC)
pretence
prevalence, prevalent
prevent, preventable, preventer (*not* -or),
 preventive (*not* preventative)
price tag (*two words*)
pricey
Priestley, Jason (actor)
Primakov, Yevgeny (Russia)
Prime minister–Use for national government
 leaders except when premier or other titles –
 German chancellor – are conventional. *See*
 premier
 –Prime Minister Ellen McKay
 –the prime minister said ...
 –the Prime Minister's Office (PMO)
 –former prime minister Ellen McKay
 –prime minister-designate Ellen McKay
 –Deputy Prime Minister Ellen McKay
prime time, prime-time program
prince
 –Prince Charles, Charles, the prince; Charles,
 Prince of Wales; the Prince of Wales
 –Crown Prince Abdullah
Prince Edward Island, the Island (P.E.I.)
princess
 –Princess Anne, Anne, the princess
 –*but* the Princess of Wales or Diana (*not*
 Princess Diana)

P

Princess Patricia's Canadian Light Infantry

principal (main, most important), school principal
     –school principal Paul Chambers

principle (fundamental belief)

prison (use for federal institutions, not holding cells
     or provincial jails)
     –Oakalla prison farm

prisoner of war (PoW, PoWs)

private (Pte. Bob Lively)
     –private first class (Pte. 1st Class)

privatize, privatization

privilege

Privy Council (*uppercase*)
     –Privy Council Office (*no abbvn.*)

proactive

processor

Procter and Gamble Inc.

prodigy, prodigies, prodigious

professor, Prof. Normand Saint-Onge

program (*not* -mme), programmer, programming
     –national energy program

Prohibition (alcohol outlawed)

Promised Land

promulgate, promulgation, promulgator (*not* -er)

proofread

propaganda

propellant (*n.*), propellent (*adj.*)

propeller (*not* -or)

prophecy (*n.*), prophesy (*v.*)

Prophet, the (Muhummad in Islam)

prorogue

prospectus, prospectuses

prostate (male gland); prostrate (lying face down;
     overcome)

Protestant, Protestantism (religion)

protester (*not* -or)

province, provincial
   –province of Ontario (geography)
   –Province of Ontario bonds (corporation)
provincewide
proviso, provisos
Prud'homme, Marcel (senator)
p's and q's
psychedelic
psychiatric, psychiatrist, psychiatry
psychic
psychopath, psychopathic
psychosis, psychoses
psychosomatic
publicly (*never* publically)
Pulitzer Prize
   –a Pulitzer Prize-winning writer
pulley, pulleys
pulp mill (*two words*)
Punxsutawney, Pa.
Pusan – *Use* Busan for city in South Korea
Pushkin, Alexander
push over (*v.*), pushover (*n.*)
push up (*v.*), pushup (*n.*)
Putin, Vladimir
putt (golf)
Pygmy
pyjamas
Pyrex (trademark for heat-resistant cookware)

Q

Qantas Airways
Qatar
Q-Tips (trademark for cotton swabs on a stick)
quadriplegic
Quai d'Orsay (French Foreign Ministry)
Quakers (Society of Friends)
quandary
Qu'Appelle, Sask.
quarter-final *but* semifinal
quarter-horse
quartet
quarto, quartos
Quebec (Que.), Quebecer (*not* -ck)
Quebec City (*but* Quebec in placelines)
Québécois, Parti Québécois (PQ)
Quebecor Inc. (TSX:QBR.A)
Quebec provincial police (*lowercase, no abbvn.*)
Queen–Capitalize all references to the reigning
        monarch: the Queen, Queen of Canada
        (*not* Queen of Britain).
     Lowercase for former monarchs and for those
     of other nations except when used as a title:
     Queen Victoria *but* when Victoria was queen;
     Queen Beatrix of the Netherlands;
     the Dutch queen.
Queen Elizabeth 2 (liner), QE2
Queen Mother (Elizabeth, 1900-2002)
Queen's counsel (QC)
Queen's Park
Queen's Plate
Queen's University, Kingston, Ont.
question-and-answer, Q-and-A, Q-and-A's
questionnaire
question period (*lowercase*)
quiche Lorraine

quixotic (extravagantly chivalrous; from Don
Quixote)
Quonset (hut)
Quotidien, Le (newspaper in Chicoutimi, Que.)
Qur'an (*not* Koran)

R

rabbi, Rabbi Stuart Rosenberg

raccoon, raccoons

race, race card, racecourse, racehorse, racetrack, raceway

racked (their brains)

racket (bat used in tennis, badminton, etc.)

racquetball (game)

Radio-Canada (*hyphen*)

Radio Moscow (*but* Moscow radio)

Radio, Television Stations–Use this style: CFCF Montreal, CHUM-FM Toronto, CBC-TV. If a station uses another name, follow its style: Mix 99.9, 680News, ROBTv.

radius, radii

railway (*preferred to* railroad)
>   –*but* Long Island Rail Road

railworker

rain, raindrop, rainfall, rainforest, rainstorm

RAM (random access memory)

Ramadan

rancour *but* rancorous

Rand (*not* RAND) Worldwide

R&B (rhythm and blues)

Ranger 4 (satellite)

rapt (absorbed, intent)

rarefy, rarefied

rational (sensible)

rationale (statement of reasons)

Ratzinger, Joseph (Pope Benedict XVI)

raucous (*not* -cus)

rayon

razzmatazz (*no hyphens*)

re-, readmit, reassess, recur, recurrence, re-examine, re-enter, reinstate, reissue, reopen, reorganize, re-cover (cover again), recover (regain), re-lay (lay again), relay (pass on), reroute, rerun, re-sign (sign again), resign (quit), reunite, reuse, reusable

Reader's Digest (*not* Readers')

ready-made (*hyphen*)

reality, realization, realize (*not* -ise)

Realtor–In Canada, a trademark and must be capitalized. Not a synonym for real estate agent. It identifies members of the Canadian Real Estate Association and the (U.S.) National Association of Realtors, which includes agents or brokers, *but* also property managers, developers and other real estate professionals.

REAL Women

rearguard

rebut, refute (prove wrong; *use with care*)

recoilless

Red (Communist, *but avoid*)

Red Cross, Red Cross Society, Red Crescent –a Red Cross campaign

redneck (rustic, poor white)

Reeves, Keanu

refer, referred

referendum, referendums

Reformation

reformatory, Guelph reformatory

refuel, refuelled

refute, rebut (prove wrong; *use with care*)

reggae

regiment, 24th Regiment

regimental sergeant major (Regimental Sgt. Maj.) –regimental sergeants major (*no abbvn.*)

Regina Leader-Post

region, Peel Region

registered education savings plan (RESP)

registered retirement savings plan (RRSP)

R

reign (rule), rein (leather strap, symbol of power)

Religion–Capitalize names of religions and denominations.

 –American Lutheran Church
 –Anglican Church of Canada
 –Baha'i faith
 –Buddhism, Buddhist
 –Church of Christ, Scientist (also Christian Science Church)
 –Church of Jesus Christ of Latter-day Saints
 –Greek Orthodox Church
 –Hinduism, Hindu
 –Islam, Muslim
 –Jehovah's Witnesses
 –Judaism (Orthodox, Reform, Conservative)
 –Pentecostal Assembly
 –Presbyterian Church in Canada
 –Roman Catholic Church
 –Seventh-day Adventist
 –Ukrainian Orthodox Church
 –United Church of Canada

relinquish

R.E.M. (musical group)

Remembrance Day (Nov. 11)

reminiscent

removable (*not* -eable)

remuneration

Renaissance (historic period), a renaissance of painting   (general sense)

renowned

repechage (rowing)

repel, repellent

repent, repentance, repentant

repertoire, repertory

representative

 –Representative Chris Flynn (D-Mass.)

–Representative Robert Brown (R-Calif.)
reprieve
republic, Fifth Republic
    –Republic of Ireland
    –the Irish republic
republican (philosophical attitude)
Republican (party or member)
    –Senator John Smith (R-Calif.)
    –Representative Mary Brown (R-Ohio)
    –Republican party (U.S.)
requiem, requiem mass
research and development, R&D (*no periods*)
reserve (*preferred to* reservation for aboriginal lands in
    Canada), the Chippewa reserve
re-sign (sign again), resign (quit)
resistance, resistibility, resistible (*not* -able)
respectability, respectable
restaurateur (*not* restauranteur)
resumé
resuscitate
retired, retired brigadier Pat Turner
Reuters, Reuters news agency
reverend
    –Rev. Alan Cross (Protestant and RC;
    Cross *on second reference*)
reverse, reversible
revolution, American Revolution
revolutions per minute (r.p.m.)
Reye's syndrome
Rh (for Rhesus) factor, Rh positive, Rh negative
rhinoceros (*sing.* and *pl.*)
Rhode Island (R.I.)
Rhodes Scholar, Scholarship
rhododendron
Rice, Condoleezza
Richler, Mordecai (author, 1931-2001)

R

Richter scale
Richthofen, Baron von (Red Baron, 1892-1918)
ricochet, ricocheted
Rideau Hall
rifleman (*no abbvn.*)
        –Rifleman Andrew Coates
right, right field, right-fielder, right wing,
        right-winger; right-field wall, right-handed
pitcher, right-wing politician (*adj., hyphen*)
        right-handed, right-hander (*hyphen*)
rigor mortis
rigour *but* rigorous
ringtone (*one word*)
Rio de Janeiro
rip off (*v.*), ripoff (*n.*)
river, St. Lawrence River
Riyadh
RJR-Macdonald Inc. – now JTI-Macdonald Corp.
Road–Capitalize when used with names,
        abbreviate in numbered street addresses.
        –along Kingston Road
        –10 Scott Rd. E.
roadblock (*one word*), road map (*two words*)
ROBTv (specialty channel)
Rock, the (informal for Newfoundland or
Gibraltar)
Rockefeller Center
rock 'n' roll
rococo
Rodrigue (given name – *not* -que)
Rogers Centre, Toronto (formerly SkyDome)
Rogers Communications Inc. (TSX:RCI.NV.B)
        –Rogers Cable
        –Rogers Media
        –Rogers Video
        –Rogers Wireless

–Rogers Yahoo (high-speed Internet)
Rogers Pass, B.C.
rollcall (*one word*)
Rollerblades (trademark for in-line skates),
    Rollerblading (*but use* in-line skating)
roller-coaster, roller derby, roller-skate (*v.*),
    roller skates
rollover (*n.*)
Rolls-Royce Ltd., a Rolls-Royce
Rolodex
roly-poly (*hyphen*)
ROM (read only memory)
Roma (*preferred to* Gypsy)
Roman Catholic (Roman may be dropped only if
    reference is obvious)
Romanesque
Romania (*not* Rumania)
Roman Numerals–Use roman numerals to indicate
    sequence for people and animals and in
    proper names where specified. Otherwise
    prefer arabic numerals as easier to grasp.
    –Pope Benedict XVI, Henry VIII, The
    Godfather, Part II
roman numerals, type
roof, roofs
room, Room 4, Oak Room
    –in the assembly room
Rorschach test
Rosh Hashanah
Rothmans Inc. (TSX:ROC)
Rothschild
Rottweiler
roundup (*n.*), round up (*v.*)
Royal Air Force (Britain)
royal assent
Royal Bank of Canada

R

Royal Canadian Air Force (until 1968)
Royal Canadian Legion
  –the legion announced ...
  –parade of legionnaires
Royal Canadian Mint, the mint
Royal Canadian Mounted Police (RCMP)
  –RCMP musical ride
  –the Mounties
Royal Canadian Navy (until 1968)
royal commission – *See commission*
Royal Family (British), royal family (other nations)
Royal Ontario Museum (ROM, *but avoid)*
royal tour, visit
royalty
Roy Thomson Hall (Toronto)
r.p.m. (revolutions per minute)
RRSP (registered retirement savings plan)
ruble
rumour
runner-up, runners-up
run-off, run-up
rural route
  –RR 2, Newmarket
rush hour, rush-hour traffic
Russia
Rwanda
RV (for recreational vehicle)
Ryerson University (Toronto)

'S – To denote the possessive add 's to singular and plural nouns not ending in "s": mother's purse, women's shoes, alumni's gifts. Add it to singular nouns ending in "s" to indicate a sis or siz sound: the boss's secretary, Strauss's waltzes, Duplessis's cabinet. But names ending with an -iz sound and classical names ending in "s" often take the apostrophe only: Bridges' ideas, Socrates' plays.

Sabbath

saccharin (*n*.), saccharine (*adj.*)

sacrilegious

Saddam Hussein (Saddam *in second reference*)

Sadler's Wells Ballet

Sailboats–Capitalize names of classes of racing and pleasure craft.

–Tornado, International Europe

St-, Ste-, St.–Use abbreviations in federal and provincial names of political ridings. Use St. for male and female saints: St. Peter, St. Anne.

St. Bernard (dog)

St. Catharines, Ont.

St. Catharines Standard

Ste-Catherine Street (Montreal)

St. Denis, Brent (politician)

St-Hilaire, Caroline (politician)

St-Hyacinthe

St. James's Palace (London)

St-Jean-Baptiste Day (June 24, also Fête nationale)

St-Jean, Que.

Saint John, N.B.

St. John Ambulance

St. John of Jerusalem, Most Venerable Order of the Hospital of (usually Order of St. John)

St. John River (N.B.)

St. John's, N.L.

St-Laurent, Louis

St. Lawrence Seaway, the seaway
    –St. Lawrence Seaway Authority
    –St. Lawrence Seaway Development Corp.
    (U.S.)

St. Marguerite Bourgeoys (Canada's first woman
    saint, 1620-1700)

St. Martin-in-the-Fields Church (London)
    –Academy of St. Martin-in-the-Fields

Saint Mary's University (Halifax)

St. Marys, Ont.

Sainte-Marie, Buffy (singer-composer)

St. Petersburg (formerly Leningrad)

St-Pierre-Miquelon (islands)
    –St-Pierre (capital city)

St. Thomas Times-Journal

St. Valentine's Day, Valentine's Day (Feb. 14)
    –*but* a valentine (card)

salability, salable (*not* -eable)

Salchow, triple Salchow (figure-skating jump)

salmonella

SALT (for strategic arms limitation talks)

Salvadoran

Salvation Army, the Army, a Salvationist

salvo, salvos (*pl.*)

SAM (for surface-to-air missile)

Samaritan, Good

Sanaa, Yemen

sanatorium, sanatoriums

sanctimonious

Sanforized (trademark for material that won't
    shrink)

San Francisco 49ers (*no apostrophe*)

Sanka (trademark for a decaffeinated coffee)

S

sapper (*no abbvn.*)
   –Sapper John Flynn
Sarajevo
Saran Wrap (trademark for a plastic film)
SARS (severe acute respiratory syndrome, *OK in
      first reference*)
Saskatchewan (Sask.)
Saskatchewan (*not* Regina) Roughriders (*one word*)
Saskatchewan Party
   –Sask. Party *OK if abbreviation needed*
saskatoon (berry)
Saskatoon StarPhoenix
sasquatch (mysterious ape-like creature)
Satan, satanic, Satanism
satellite – *See Space*
Sault Ste. Marie, Ont. and Mich.
      –the Sault (*not* the Soo)
      –*but* Soo Greyhounds hockey team
Sauvageau, Benoit (politician)
Savile Row (London)
saviour, Saviour (Christ)
savory (herb)
savour, savoury (flavour)
saxophone
scare, scary, scarier
scarf, scarves
scarlet fever
Scene 2, the second scene
sceptic – *Use* skeptic
Schafer, R. Murray (composer)
Schefferville, Que.
schizophrenia, schizophrenic
scholar, Rhodes Scholar, Scholarship
School–Capitalize when using proper name.
      –Leaside High School
      –Our Lady of Sorrows School

S

- –London School of Economics
- –University of Toronto Schools
- –Royal York Academy *(proper name)* but Royal York high school
- –Kingslake Public School *(proper name)* but Kingslake elementary school
- –the McGill medical school
- –day school, private school
- –Sunday school
- –school board, schoolbook, schoolboy, school bus, schoolgirl, school guard, schoolmarm, school teacher, school trustee, schoolyard

Schumann, Robert (composer, 1810-1856)

Schwarzenegger, Arnold

Scotch Tape (trademark for sticky tape)

scotch whisky

Scotiabank, Scotiabank Group (TSX:BNS)
- –Bank of Nova Scotia (legal name)
- –ScotiaMcLeod (retail brokerage)
- –Scotia Capital Inc. (corporate investment arm)

Scots or Scottish (*not* Scotch)

Scotsman (*not* Scotchman)

scout
- –Scouts Canada
- –the Scouts (association)
- –a scout
- –eagle scout (U.S.)
- –Beaver
- –Cub
- –Chief Scout's Award
- –Venturer Scout, Venturers

Scrabble (trademark for a word game)

Screech (rum)

Scripture (Bible)

S-curve
scuttlebutt (*no hyphen*)
Sea–Capitalize when preceding or following the
    specific term.
    –Sea of Galilee
    –Black Sea
Sea-Doo (trademark for a brand of personal
    watercraft)
Seafarers International Union of Canada (SIU)
seaman
    –able seaman (*no abbvn.*)
    –leading seaman (*no abbvn.*)
    –ordinary seaman (*no abbvn.*)
Sears Canada Inc. (TSX:SCC)
    –a Sears store, Sears
Seasons–Lowercase for spring, summer, fall or
    autumn, winter
season's greetings
seatbelt (*one word*)
SEATO (for Southeast Asia Treaty Organization)
seaway, St. Lawrence Seaway
    –St. Lawrence Seaway Authority
    –St. Lawrence Seaway Development Corp.
second lieutenant (2nd Lieut. Marie Demers)
Second World War (*not* World War II)
secretary general (*no hyphen*)
Section 23, Sec. 5
Security Council (UN)
seder
Seeing Eye (trademark for guide dog)
seigneur, seigniory
semi, semi-annual, semicircle, semicolon, semifinal
    (*but* quarter-final), semifinalist, semi-invalid,
    semi-official, semitransparent, semitropical,
    semi-weekly
Semite, Semitism, anti-Semitism

S

Senate (national legislature)
>–the university senate

senator (*no abbvn.*)
>–Senator John McLean (D–Mass.)
>–former senator Robert de Cotret

senior chief petty officer (*no abbvn.*)

sensual (gratifying to the body, especially sexually), sensuous (appealing to the senses, especially through beauty)

separate school, school board

Sept. 11 (day of terrorist attacks in United States; *not* September 11), 9-11

Serb (*n.*), Serbian (*adj.*)

Serbia and Montenegro (formerly Yugoslavia)
>–SERBIA-MONTENEGRO (placelines)

sergeant (Sgt. Margaret Bonotto)
>–staff sergeant (Staff Sgt. Margaret Bonotto)

sergeant-at-arms

sergeant first class (Sgt. 1st Class)

sergeant major (Sgt. Maj. Fred Tylee)
>–regimental sergeant major (Regimental Sgt. Maj.)
>–sergeants major (*pl.*)

series (*generally lowercase*)
>–*but* World Series, the Series, Little League World Series

set up (*v.*), setup (*n.*)

Seventh-day Adventist

7Up (soft drink)
>–Seven-Up (corporate references)

severe acute respiratory syndrome (SARS *OK in first reference)*

sewage (waste), sewerage (drainage)

Sex and the City (TV show, *not* Sex in the City)

sextet

sexually transmitted disease (STD *but avoid*)

shakable (*not* -eable)
shake down (*v.*), shakedown (*n.* and *adj.*)
shake out (v.), shakeout (*n.* and *adj.*)
Shakespeare, Shakespearean
shake up (*v.*), shakeup (*n.*)
shaky, shakier, shakiness
shalom (greeting)
shaman, shamans (*pl.*), Shamanism
shanghai (*v.*), shanghaied, shanghaiing
Shangri-La
shanty, shanties
Sharansky, Natan
Shariah (Muslim code of religious law)
Shaw Communications Inc. (TSX:SJR.NV.B)
sheik (*not* shiek)
shellac, shellacking
Shell Canada Ltd. (TSX:SHC)
shemozzle (commotion)
sheriff, Sheriff Anton Gerber
Sheshatshiu, Labrador (formerly Sheshatsheit)
Shiite Muslim
Shippagan, N.B. (*not* Shippegan)
shipwreck (*no hyphen*)
Shirleys Bay, Ont. (*no apostrophe*)
shish kebab
shiva
shivaree (friendly invasion of newlyweds' home)
shlemiel (foolish, unlucky person)
shlep (to drag)
shlock (shoddy)
shmaltz (sentimentality)
shmo (a fool, a clumsy person)
shmooz (chat)
shnook (a patsy)
shnorrer (a moocher, panhandler)
shoo-in

shoot out (*v.*), shootout (*n.*)
Shoppers Drug Mart Corp. (TSX:SC)
shoptalk
short list (*n.*) shortlist (*v.*)
shortwave (broadcasting)
shotgun (*one word*)
shot put (*two words*)
show, flower show, horse show
shtick (a gimmick; clowning)
shut out (*v.*), shutout (*n.*)
siamese twins (*use* joined twins or description:
     babies born attached at the hips)
side-effect
Sidney, B.C.
SIDS (*but use* sudden infant death syndrome *in
     first reference*)
siege (*not* -ei-)
sight, sightseeing, sightseer
signal, signalled, signaller
signalman (no abbvn.)
     –Signalman William O'Callaghan
Sikh, the Sikh religion
Siksika (aboriginal band)
silhouette
Silicon Valley
silo, silos
Simoniz (trademark for a car wax)
Sinn Fein
sinus, sinuses
siphon (*not* syphon)
sir, Sir John Jones; Sir John *or preferably* Jones *in
     second reference*
sirocco (Italian name for Sahara wind)
sitcom (TV situation comedy)
Sites–*See Locations*
sizable (*not* -eable)

skating, figure skating, ice skating, speed skating
    (*hyphenate when used adjectivally*)
skeptic, skeptical, skepticism (*not* sc-)
ski, skier, skis, skiing
Ski-Doo (snowmobile trademark)
skid row (*not* road)
skilful
skulduggery
SkyDome – *See Rogers Centre*
slaughterhouse
Slovakia
small-c conservative
smallmouth (bass)
Smallwood, Joey (*not* Joseph, 1900-1991)
smart-alec
Smiths Falls, Ont. (*no apostrophe)*
Smithsonian Institution (*not* Institute)
smoky (*not* smokey)
smorgasbord
smoulder
snakehead (human smuggler)
snob, snobbery, snobbish, snobbishness
snow, snowblower, snowfall, snowflake,
    snowflurries, snowstorm
Snowbirds (Canadian Forces flying team)
snowbirds (Canadians who winter in the South)
snowmobile (*one word)*
snowshoe, snowshoer
s.o.b.
sober
Sobeys Inc. (TSX:SBY)
Social Credit party
Social Crediter (*not* -or)
socialism, socialist (philosophical attitude)
Socialist (party or member)

Société franco-manitobaine, la
society, Audubon Society
Socred (*n.* and *adj.*)
softpedal (*not* -peddle)
soft-spoken (*hyphen*)
software
softy, softies
Solberg, Monte (politician)
Soleil, Le (Quebec)
solicitor general, solicitors general
solo, solos
soluble
Solzhenitsyn, Alexander
Somali (*n.*), Somalian (*adj.*)
sombre (*not* -er)
some, someday, someplace, somebody,
      somebodies, somehow, someone, something,
      at some time (*two words*), sometime (*adv.*;
      adj.), somewhat, somewhere
Somers, Harry (composer, 1925-99)
somersault
soprano, sopranos
SOS (*no periods*)
Sotheby's Canada Inc.
    –Sotheby's for short
South–Capitalize regions *but not* their derivatives.
    Lowercase mere direction or position.
    –the South (region of Canada, United States,
    etc.)
    –a southerner
    –Southern California
    –Southern Canada
    –southern Canadian markets
    –southern prices
    –south of the border
    –to go south

–the Deep South (U.S.)
–a southern accent
–southern states (U.S.)
–The South lost to the North.
–the southern army
–the South Pacific
–southern Ireland

South Asia, South Asian (*not* East India, East Indian)

South Carolina (S.C.)

South Dakota (S.D.)

southeast (*one word*)
–Southeast Asia (region), southeast Asian (*adj.*)
–Southeast Asia Treaty Organization (SEATO)

Southern Canada, southern Canadian weather

southern France

Southern Hemisphere

southern Ontario

southern states (U.S.)

South Pole, the Pole

sou'wester (waterproof hat)

sovereigntist (*not* sovereignist)

sovereignty-association

Soviet Union, former (Union of Soviet Socialist Republics, U.S.S.R.)

soybean, soy sauce

Space–Use arabic numerals for spacecraft and launch vehicles: Sputnik 1, Apollo 11, Gemini 5, Alouette 2. *But* Anik A, Anik B.

Spanish Civil War

Spartan

Speaker–Capitalize in all references to avoid ambiguity.
–Speaker Martha Lim, the Speaker

  –deputy Speaker Glenn Eckert, the deputy
   Speaker, former Speaker
spectre (*not* -er)
speech from the throne
speed skater, speed skating
spellbinder (*no hyphen*)
spellcheck, spellchecker *(one word)*
sphinx (winged monster)
Sphinx (representation near pyramids)
Spider-Man (comic, movie)
Spielberg, Steven
spina bifida
spin off (*v.*), spinoff (*n.* and *adj.*)
splendour
spoonful, spoonfuls
sport utility vehicle (*not* sports; SUV)
spring (season)
squadron leader (*no abbvn.*)
Squid-Jiggin' Ground, the (Newfoundland
  ballad)
Srebrenica (Bosnia)
Sri Lanka, Sri Lankan
  –Sri Lanka Freedom party
SS (steamship)
SS (Schutzstaffel, Nazi elite guard)
stadium, stadiums
staff, staffs (poles), staves (music)
staff inspector, Staff Insp. Albert Dupont
staff sergeant (Staff Sgt.)
Stalin, Josef (1879-1953)
stampede, Calgary Stampede, the Stampede
Standard & Poor's Corp.
  –S&P/TSX composite index
standardbred, thoroughbred
standard time
  –eastern, central, mountain standard time

–Atlantic, Pacific daylight time

–MST, EDT (*not* EDST)

stand by (*v.*), standby (*n.*), standbys

stand in (*v.*), stand-in (*n.*)

stand off (*v.*), standoff (*n.*)

Standoff, Alta.

stand out (*v.*), standout (*n.*)

standup (*n.* and *adj.*)

Stanley Cup

Star (*not* Star!) specialty channel

Stars and Stripes

startup (*n* and *adj.*)

state, New York state (geog.)

> –State of New York (corp.)
> –*but* in the state of New York
> –state of the union message

Station–Capitalize as important building *but* not when known by name of railway or town.

> –Union Station
> –the Via Rail station
> –Mimico station

stationary (not moving)

stationery (writing materials)

Statistics Canada (*not* StatsCan *except in headlines*)

STD (*use* sexually transmitted disease)

steelworker

Stefansson, Vilhjalmur (explorer, 1879-1962)

Steinem, Gloria (feminist)

Stelco Inc. (Steel Co. of Canada Ltd., TSX:STE)

Stephenson, Sir William (1896-1989)

stepdaughter, stepson, stepmother, stepfather *but* step-parent

stepping-stone (*hyphen*)

Stetson (trademark)

S

still life, still lifes
stimulus, stimuli
stock exchange, Toronto Stock Exchange
stock market
stockpile (*one word*)
STOL (short takeoff and landing; *avoid*)
Stone Age
Stoney band (Alberta Indians), Stoneys
Stoney Creek, Ont. and N.B.
stony (*not* stoney)
Stony Lake (near Peterborough, Ont.)
Stony Mountain, Man.
Stony Plain, Alta.
storey (building), storeys
storm, hailstorm, rainstorm, snowstorm
strafe, strafing
Strahl, Chuck (politician)
straightforward (*no hyphen*)
Strait–Capitalize when used with names.
    –Strait of Juan de Fuca
    –Georgia Strait
straitjacket
straitlaced
stratagem, stratagems
Stratas, Teresa (soprano)
strategic arms limitation talks (SALT)
    –SALT I, SALT II
Stratford Beacon Herald
Stratford Festival (*not* Stratford Shakespearean
    Festival)
    –*but* Stratford Shakespearean Festival
    Foundation of Canada
Stratford upon Avon (Britain)
    –STRATFORD UPON AVON (in
    placelines)
stratum, strata

streamline (*one word*)

Street–Capitalize when used with names; abbreviate in numbered street addresses.
–Bay Street, Wall Street
–along Queen Street East
–10 Queen St. E.
–*but* 10 Downing Street (official residence)

streetcar (*one word*)

Streisand, Barbra

streptococcus, streptococci
–*but* strep throat

strikebound (*no hyphen*)

strikebreaker (generally editorial; *use advisedly*)

striptease

strongman

strontium-90

Styrofoam (trademark for a plastic foam)

suave, suavely, suaveness, suavily, suavities

subcommittee (*no hyphen*)

subcompact

sub judice (*two words, but avoid*)

sub-lieutenant (Sub-Lieut.)

submachine-gun

subpoena (*n.* and *v.*), subpoenas, subpoenaed, subpoenaing

subtle, subtlety, subtleties

succinct, succinctly

sudden infant death syndrome (SIDS OK *in second reference*)

suffragan (bishop)

Sukkot (Jewish festival)

sulfa drugs

sulphide, sulphite, sulphur

Sum 41 (performing group)

summer (season)

summerfallow

Summerside Journal-Pioneer
summit, summit conference (heads of government)
summons, summonses
summonsed (to appear in court)
sun
Suncor Energy Inc. (TSX:SU)
      –Sunoco (retail brand in Canada)
Sunni Muslim
Super Bowl
supercilious (*not* -silious)
superintendent, Supt. Herman Frank
supermarket (*one word*)
supersede
suppress, suppression, suppressor
supremacist (*not* supremist)
Supreme Court (federal, provincial, state)
Sûreté du Québec (*prefer* Quebec provincial police)
Suriname
Suzuki, David (geneticist)
SUV (sport utility vehicle)
swap (*not* swop)
SWAT (special weapons and tactics) team
sweatshirt
sweepstake
sweeten, sweetener, sweetening
Sydney, N.S., and Australia, *but* Sidney, B.C.
Sydney Cape Breton Post
Sydney Steel Corp. (Sysco)
syllabus, syllabuses
symbol, symbolize
symmetrical, symmetry
symphony, Tchaikovsky's Fourth Symphony
symposium, symposiums
synagogue, Holy Blossom Synagogue
syndrome, Reye's, Down
synod, Anglican synod, general synod

    –Lutheran Church – Missouri Synod (denom.)

    –Orthodox Holy synod (Istanbul)

syphilis

Syrah (grape)

syrup (*not* sirup)

Sysco (Sydney Steel Corp.)

T

T, *as in* to a T
Tabasco (trademark for a hot sauce)
tableau, tableaus
taekwondo (*one word)*
tai chi (*two words*)
Taipei
Tajikistan, Tajik
take off (*v.*), takeoff. (*n.*)
take out (*v.*), takeout (*n.*)
take over (*v.*), takeover (*n.*)
Taliban
tangelo, tangelos
tank, M-60, PT-76, Leopard 1
targeted
tariff, Tariff Act
    –General Agreement on Tariffs and Trade
    (GATT)
tarsands *(one word)*
Taser (weapon)
task force (military term; *avoid overuse*)
Tass – *See Itar-Tass*
tassel, tasselled
tattoo, tattooed
T-ball
T-cell
Tchaikovsky, Peter (1840-1893)
TD Bank Financial Group (Toronto-Dominion Bank
    and its subsidiaries)
    –TD Canada Trust (banking)
    –TD Waterhouse (investing)
teammate (*no hyphen*)
Teamsters union (*acceptable in all references for*
    International Brotherhood of Teamsters,
    Chauffeurs, Warehousemen and Helpers of
    America), a teamster (member of the union)
    tear gas (*two words*)

T

technical sergeant (Tech. Sgt.)
Technicolor (trademark for a process of making
        colour movies)
Teck Cominco Ltd. (TSX:TEK.SV.B)
teenage (*adj.*), teenager, teens
teenybopper
teepee
teetotal, teetotaller, teetotalism
Teflon (trademark for a non-stick coating)
Tehran
telecommunication
Telefilm Canada
Telephone numbers–Use hyphen, not brackets or
        spaces to break up: 1-519-228-6262,
        1-800-268-9237.
TelePrompTer (trademark)
Telex (trade name)
telltale (*no hyphen*)
Telus Corp. (TSX:T)
Temagami, Ont. (*not* Tim-)
Témiscaming, Que. (town)
Témiscamingue (Que. county, electoral district)
Ten Commandments
        –Second Commandment
tendency (*not* -ancy), tendencies
tendon, Achilles tendon, *but* tendinitis
ten-gallon hat
Tennant, Veronica (ballet)
Tennessee (Tenn.)
tenpins (bowling)
tenterhooks (*not* tender-)
Teresa, Mother (1910-1997)
terminus, terminuses
Terry Fox Run
testament, Old Testament
Test match (cricket, rugby)

 –England-Australia Test match
 –the Test
Texas (*no abbvn.*)
textbook
thalidomide
Thanksgiving Day (Canada, second Monday in
 October; U.S., last Thursday in November)
The–Capitalize at the beginning of the titles of
 books, magazines, movies, TV programs,
 songs, paintings and other compositions.
 Don't capitalize at the start of the names of
 almanacs, the Bible, directories,
 encyclopedias, gazetteers and handbooks.
The Associated Press (AP)
 –The Associated Press says ...
 –*but* the Associated Press reporter
Theatre–Capitalize as important buildings.
 –National Arts Centre
 –Princess of Wales Theatre
theatregoer
The Canadian Press (CP)
 –The Canadian Press says ...
 –*but* the Canadian Press reporter
The Hague
the (*lowercase*) Netherlands
 –UTRECHT, Netherlands (placeline)
The Pas, Man.
therapeutic
thesis, theses
the West Indies
think-tank
Third World
Thompson, Greg (politician)
Thompson, Myron (politician)
Thomson Corp. (TSX:TOC)
 –Thomson, Ken

Thomson, R.H. (actor)
Thomson, Tom (painter, 1877-1917)
thoroughbred, standardbred
Thousand Islands (Ontario)
3-D
Three Wise Men
threshold
throne speech, speech from the throne
Thunder Bay Chronicle-Journal
Tiananmen Square
tick-tack-toe (game)
tidbit
tie, tying
tiebreaker (game)
tie up (*v.*), tie-up (*n.*)
till, until, *not* 'til
time, daylight, standard
      –eastern daylight time (EDT)
      –Pacific standard time (PST)
      –7 a.m., 6 p.m., 12:30 p.m.
Time magazine
Times (of London), the
time-slot
Tim Hortons (*no apostrophe*)
      –a Tim Hortons shop
Timiskaming (Ontario lake and district)
Timiskaming-Cochrane (federal riding in Ontario)
Timiskaming reserve (Quebec)
Timorese (*n.* and *adj.*)
Titles–Capitalize formal titles when preceding
      names, not when following or when set off by
      commas: Judge John Jones; a judge, John
      Jones, spoke. But lowercase titles used with
      former, one-time, -elect, designate and similar
      adjectives, as former president Bill Clinton,
      former prime minister Jean Chretien, prime

minister-designate Julie Smith. Lowercase mere occupation (GM president John Wong, bus driver Ron Brown) and in sport stories (captain Donna Hooper).

Tkachuk, David (senator)

TNT (trinitrotoluene)

T.O. (nickname for Toronto)

to a T

toboggan

tomato, tomatoes

ton (2,000 pounds), long ton (2,240 pounds), tonne (1,000 kilograms or 2,204.62 pounds)
> – *Use* ton, not tonne, in colloquial references (he weighed a ton; fell like a ton of bricks).

toonie, toonies ($2 coin)

top-notch (*adj.*)

tornado, tornadoes

Toronto-Dominion Bank – *See TD Bank Financial Group*

Toronto 1 (TV channel)

Toronto St. Michael's Majors (hockey team)

Toronto Stock Exchange, TSX
> –S&P/TSX composite index
> –TSX Group Inc. (corporation)
> –TSX Venture Exchange

Torstar Corp. (TSX:TS.NV.B)

total, totalled

Touch-Tone (trademark for push-button dialling)

tourniquet

tower, CN Tower, Eiffel Tower

town, Town of Elmira (corp.)
> –*but* in the town of Elmira

township, Wilmot Township
> –*but* in the township of Wilmot

Toys "R" Us

trademark, trade name

traffic, trafficker, trafficking
traitor, traitorous
tranquillity
tranquillizer
TransAlta Corp. (TSX:TA)
transatlantic, transpacific
Trans-Canada Highway
TransCanada Corp. (TSX:TRP)
    –TransCanada PipeLines Ltd.
    (TSX:TCA.PR.X)
transcontinental (*no hyphen*)
Transcontinental Inc. (TSX:TCL.SV.A)
trans fat (*two words*)
transfer, transferred
Transkei (former homeland state in South Africa)
translator (*not* -er)
transpacific
Transport Canada
Transportation Safety Board
trauma, traumas, traumatic
travel, traveller, traveller's cheques
Treasury Board
treaty, Columbia River Treaty
    –Treaty 6 (*not* Six)
Treehouse TV
tremor
trendsetter, trendsetting
Tribune, La (newspaper in Sherbrooke, Que.)
Trilon Financial Corp. – *See Brascan Corp.*
Trimark Financial Corp.
triple-A rating (bonds, baseball)
Triple Crown (horse racing)
triple-decker
Triple-E Senate
TriStar (Lockheed aircraft)
Trivial Pursuit (trademark board game)

T

Trois-Rivières, Que.

trooper (military, *no abbvn.*), trouper (a staunch colleague – a "real trouper")

Trophy–Capitalize specific names.
  –Vézina Trophy
  –a championship trophy

Trudeau, Alexandre (*preferred to* Sacha)

Trudeau, Pierre Elliott (1919-2000)

Truman, Harry S. (1884-1972)

trustee, trustee Joanne Rocci

Tsawwassen, B.C.

T-shirt

tsunami (wave), tsunamis *(pl.)*

Tsuu T'ina Nation (aboriginal band)

TSX (Toronto Stock Exchange)
  –TSX Venture Exchange (junior exchange)
  –S&P/TSX composite index

Tube (London subway; also Underground)

tug of war (*no hyphens*)

Tuktoyaktuk, N.W.T.

tumour *but* tumorous

tune-up (*n.*)

tupek (Inuit equivalent of teepee, wigwam)

tuque (knitted cap; otherwise toque)

Turin, Italy

turkey, turkeys

Turkmenistan

Turp, Daniel (politician)

turtleneck sweater (*no hyphen*)

Tussaud's, Madame (wax museum in London)
  –*but* Louis Tussaud's Waxworks (Niagara Falls, Ont.)

Tutankhamen

Tutor (training jet)

TVA Group Inc. (TSX:TVA.NV.B)

TV dinner

TV Land (specialty channel)
TVOntario, TVO
tween, tweens (usually eight- to 14-year-olds)
Twelfth Night
Twelve Apostles, the
20th Century Fox *(no hyphen)*
two, twos
tying *(not* tieing)
typeface
Type 1, Type 2 diabetes
typhoon Alice

U

U-boat
UFO(s) (unidentified flying object(s))
U.K. (*use periods*)
Ukraine (*not* the Ukraine)
Ukrainian
ultimatum, ultimatums
ultrasound
Ultrasuede (trademark for a mock suede)
ultra vires (beyond the powers, *but avoid*)
umiak (Inuit open boat)
Umlaut–Indicate in German names by placing
      letter "e" after vowel affected.
         –Goebbels for Göbbels
         –Duesseldorf for Düsseldorf
unabomber (Theodore Kaczynski)
unchristian, *but* non-Christian
unco-operative
unco-ordinated
underprivileged
undersecretary (*one word*)
underway
unforeseen
unforgivable (*not* -eable)
uninterested (not interested), disinterested (impartial)
UNICEF (*OK in first reference*)
union, state of the union message
Union Jack
Union Nationale
Union of Soviet Socialist Republics, former (U.S.S.R.,
      Soviet Union)
United Appeal campaign
United Church of Canada
United Kingdom–England, Scotland, Wales and
      Northern Ireland. But use "British
      government" and such in preference to

"United Kingdom government."
-U.K. *(periods)*
United Nations (UN)
    –Food and Agriculture Organization of the
    United Nations (FAO, *but avoid*)
    –General Assembly
    –International Bank for Reconstruction and
    Development (World Bank)
    –International Civil Aviation Organization
    (ICAO)
    –International Court of Justice (*no abbvn.*)
    –International Labour Organization (ILO)
    –International Monetary Fund (IMF)
    –Office for the Co-ordination of
    Humanitarian Affairs (OCHA, *but avoid*)
    –Security Council
    –UN Children's Fund (UNICEF)
    –UN Educational, Scientific and
    Cultural Organization (UNESCO)
    –UN High Commissioner for Refugees
    –World Food Program
    –World Health Organization (WHO)
University–Capitalize the names of universities
    and colleges.
    –Memorial University
    –Simon Fraser University
    –Cariboo College
    –Regis College
    Lowercase departments, programs and
    courses.
    –political science department
    –native studies course
    –faculty of education
University Degrees–Lowercase except when
    abbreviated.
    –bachelor of arts (BA), a bachelor's degree

U

–master of arts (MA)
–master of science (M.Sc.)
–doctor of philosophy (PhD)
Avoid using unfamiliar abbreviations for
degrees.
Unknown Soldier
unmistakable (*not* -eable)
unshakable (*not* -eable)
unwieldy
Upper Canada (region; name for Ontario 1791-
1841)
uppercase (*n.* and *v.*)
upper house, chamber
Upstate New York
URL (uniform or universal resource locator)
US (use only with dollar figures: $550 US)
usable (*not* useable)
usage (*not* useage)
USAir, US Airways Group Inc.
USA Today
usurer, usurious, usury
Utah (no abbvn.)
Utopia
–*but* a utopia
–utopian
U-turn
Uzbekistan, Uzbek (*n.* and *adj.*)

vacillate
vacuum
Val-d'Isère
valentine (card)
    –*but* Valentine's Day
Valhalla
Valium (trademark for a tranquillizer)
Valkyrie
valley, Fraser Valley
valour *but* valorous
Van, Von–When lowercase in names, capitalize only at start of sentences. Van in Vietnamese names is uppercase.
Vancouver Grizzlies (former basketball team)
Van Doo (nickname of Quebec's Royal 22nd Regiment)
    –Van Doos (personnel of the regiment)
    –Van Doo (one member)
van Gogh, Vincent (1853-1890)
Vanier, Georges (1888-1967)
vapour, vapourish *but* vaporous
Vaseline (trademark for a petroleum jelly)
Vatican II, Second Vatican Council
vaudeville
V-chip (television)
VCR (*OK in first reference* for video cassette recorder)
Veda (scripture of Hinduism)
VE-Day, VJ-Day (for Victory in Europe Day, Victory in Japan Day)
Velcro (trademark)
venetian blind
ventilator (*not* respirator)
veranda (*not* -ah)
verbatim (*not* -um)
Vermilion, Alta.

V

Vermont (Vt.)

Versus–Use the abbreviation vs. only in sports schedules, agate and the names of court cases.

vertebra, vertebrae

veterinarian

Vézina Trophy

Viagra (impotence drug)

Via Rail (*not* VIA)

vice (bad habit), vise (clamp)

vice-admiral (*no abbvn.*)

vice-president
>   –U.S. Vice-President James Smith
>   –former U.S. vice-president Al Gore
>   –GM vice-president Joan Arthur

vice versa (*two words*)

vichyssoise

vicious

Vickers, Jon (tenor)

Victoria Cross (VC)

Victoria Times Colonist

video, videocassette, videocassette recorder (VCR acceptable *in first reference*), videotape, video game

Videotron (cable provider owned by Quebecor Inc.)

vie, *but* vying

Vietnam, Vietnamese

vigour, vigorous

vilify

village, Village of Bridgeport (corp.)
>   –*but* in the village of Bridgeport

VIP (for very important person), VIPs

Virgin (Christ's mother)

Virginia (Va.)

Virgin Islands (*no abbvn.*)

virtuoso, virtuosos
Visa (credit card)
vis-a-vis
viscount, Viscount Montgomery
viscous (sticky)
vise (clamp), vice (bad habit)
Vishnu
VisionTV (specialty channel)
vitamin B
Vizinczey, Stephen (novelist)
VJ (*not* veejay), VJs, VJing
VLT (video lottery terminal)
V-neck
vociferous
voice mail (*two words*)
Voice of Women (VoW)
voice-over-Internet protocol (VoIP *in second reference)*
Voisey's Bay (Labrador)
Voix de l'Est, La (newspaper in Granby, Que.)
volatile
volcano, volcanoes
Volkswagen
vomit, vomited, vomiting
Von, Van–When lowercase in names, capitalize
only at start of sentence except for van in
Vietnamese names, which is uppercase.
     –Kai-Uwe von Hassel (Germany)
     –Nguyen Van Hai (Vietnam)
vow (solemn oath; often misused)
vs. (abbreviation for versus, used only in sports
     schedules, agate and the names of court cases)

wacky (*not* whacky)
wagon, bandwagon, chuckwagon, station wagon
wake-up call
Walesa, Lech
walkie-talkie
Walkman (trademark for headset stereo)
walk out (*v.*), walkout (*n.*)
Walkuere, Die (Wagner opera)
wall, Berlin Wall, Great Wall of China, Wailing Wall
     (in Jerusalem; *prefer* Western Wall), Wall Street
Wal-Mart
War–Capitalize major armed conflicts.
     –Civil War (U.S.)
     –First World War (*not* World War I)
     –Persian Gulf War
     –Second World War (*not* World War II)
     –*but* a third world war
     –Six-Day War
     –Korean War
     –Vietnam War
     –Wars of the Roses
     –cod war
     –tariff war
     –Cold War (fanciful term)
Ward 2
warhorse, warlord, warmonger
Warner Bros. Entertainment (division of AOL Time
     Warner)
warrant officer (*no abbvn.*)
     –chief warrant officer
     –master warrant officer
Warsaw Pact, former
wartime
Washington, D.C.
Washington (Wash.)
WASP (white Anglo-Saxon Protestant)

Wassermann test
wastebasket
Wasylycia-Leis, Judy (politician)
watchdog
waterfowl
Waterloo, University of (*not* Waterloo University)
Waterloo Region Record; the Record, of Waterloo
    Region
water-ski, water-skiing
wavelength
web, web browser, webcam, webcast, web-enabled,
    webmaster, web page, weblog, web server,
    website *but* World Wide Web
Web Addresses–It is not necessary to include
    http://. But do include less familiar
    common forms such as ftp://. Follow upper
    and lowercase: www.cp.org.
    When a company uses its web address as its
    corporate name, capitalize the first letter:
    Amazon.com
Week–Capitalize special events: Earth Week.
weekday, weekend, weeklong (*one word*)
weird, weirdo
Welch (regiment names)
    –*but* Welsh Guards
Welland Canal
well-being (*hyphen*)
Welsh (folk, tongue)
welsh (on a bet; *avoid*)
Welshpool, N.B. (*not* Welch-)
West–Capitalize regions but not their derivatives.
    Lowercase mere direction or position.
    –the West (region of Canada or the world)
    –the richest countries in the West
    –the richest western countries
    –The West won the Grey Cup.

W

    —a westerner
    —one western MP
    —Western Canada
    —a western Canadian
    —the western Canadian provinces
    —the western provinces
    —western premiers
    —in western Manitoba
    —The snow moved west across Western Canada.
    —West Coast (region)
    —west coast (shoreline)
    —the East-West talks
    —western Europe
    —western leaders
    —western France
    —Western Hemisphere
West Bank (of the River Jordan)
West End (London theatre district)
western (movie, book)
WestJet Airlines Ltd. (TSX:WJA)
Westminster, Westminster Abbey (London), New Westminster, B.C.
Westmorland County (N.B. and England)
West Nile virus
West Virginia (W.Va.)
West, Wild
Weston, Hilary
Weyerhaeuser Co. Ltd.
W-Five
wharf, wharfs
Wheat—Capitalize varieties generally except where usage has established the lowercase; Selkirk, *but* durum.
wheelchair
whereabouts (usually takes a singular verb)

Whibley, Deryck (Sum 41)
whip, party whip John O'Neill
whisky, whiskies (*never* whiskey)
whistleblower *(no hyphen)*
Whitehorse, Yukon
White House
white paper (a report issued by government to
       provide information)
whiz, whiz-kid
whodunit (*not* -nn-)
Whycocomagh (First Nations band on Cape
       Breton)
wide (*suffix*), citywide, worldwide, provincewide,
       countrywide (*avoid* nationwide when
       countrywide is meant), Canada-wide
widescreen
wield
wiener, wiener schnitzel
Wi-Fi (wireless fidelity; prefer description such as
       wireless network *in first reference*)
wigwag *(no hyphen)*
Wild West
Wilfrid Laurier University
wilful (*not* willful)
Wimbledon tennis championships
wing commander (Wing Cmdr.)
winter (season)
Winter Olympic Games, the Winter Games,
       the Games
Wisconsin (Wis.)
wit, halfwit, halfwitted
       –at his wit's end
withdraw, withdrawal
withhold
W Network (TV)
Wojtyla, Karol (Pope John Paul II, 1978-2005)

Woman–Don't use as an adjective unless man
would be used in similar fashion
(womenswear, menswear). *Prefer* female if it
is necessary to specify sex.
–female astronaut, *not* woman astronaut
Woman's Christian Temperance Union (*not*
Women's)
womenswear, menswear
woollen, woolly
Workers Compensation Board (*no apostrophe* in
Manitoba, Prince Edward Island)
Workers' Compensation Board (*with
apostrophe* in Alberta, British Columbia,
Northwest Territories and Nunavut, Nova
Scotia, Saskatchewan)
Workers' Compensation, Health and Safety Board
(Yukon)
workforce
workload
workplace
Workplace Health, Safety and Compensation
Commission (New Brunswick,
Newfoundland and Labrador)
Workplace Safety and Insurance Board (Ontario)
world
–Old World, New World
–free world (*but avoid*)
–Third World
World Bank
World Cup (soccer)
World Health Organization (WHO)
World Series (baseball), the Series
world's fair, Montreal, New York
–Canadian World Exhibition (official name)
–Expo 67, Expo 86 (*no apostrophe*)
worldwide (*one word*)

W

World Wide Web, the web
worshippers
worthwhile
write off (*v.*), writeoff (*n.*)
wrongdoer, wrongdoing, wrongful
Wyoming (Wyo.)

X-Y-Z

X-Acto (trademark for knives)
Xbox
X chromosome, Y chromosome
Xerox (trademark for a photocopier, etc.)
Xinhua (New China news agency)
X-Files, The
X-rated (movie)
X-ray (*n.* and *v.*)
Xtreme Sports (TV specialty channel)

yahoo
Yahoo Inc. (*not* Yahoo! Inc.)
Yahweh
Yamani, Sheik Ahmed Zaki
Yangon (formerly Rangoon)
Yankee
yarmulke (skullcap)
Year, Man of the, Newsmaker of the
Yellowhead Pass
yenta
Y-Flyer (sailboat)
YMCA (Young Men's Christian Association)
yogurt
Yom Kippur
Young Offenders Act (*no apostrophe*, replaced in
        April 2003 with Youth Criminal Justice Act)
yo-yo, yo-yos
Yugoslavia – *See Serbia and Montenegro*
Yukon, the (*no abbvn.*)
        –*but* Yukon in placelines: FARO, Yukon
yule, yuletide
yuppie (young urban professional)
YWCA (Young Women's Christian Association)

Zaire (now Congo)
Zamboni (trademark for ice-surfacing machine)

Zellers (*no apostrophe*)
Zen Buddhism
zero, zeros
Zhou Enlai (1898-1976, formerly Chou En-lai)
zidovudine (HIV-AIDS drug, also called AZT)
zigzag (*no hyphen*)
Zimbabwe
Zinfandel
Zion, Zionism, Zionist
zip code (U.S.)
Znaimer, Moses (television)
zodiac
zoologist, zoology
zucchini

Numbers

Act 1, the first act
Article 8, Art. 8
behind the 8-ball
Big Five banks
Big Three automakers
Category 3
CBC Radio One, Radio Two
Cdn (used only with dollar figures: $1,386 Cdn)
Cell Block 5
cents, nine cents, 43 cents
Channel 2 (television)
Chapter 2
Chromosome 7
Cloud 9
CO2 (carbon dioxide; don't use *in first reference*)
Day 1
VIII (*no period*)
55 BC; AD 1978
49th parallel
four-by-four (four-wheel-drive vehicle)
4-for-5 (four hits in five at-bats)
4-H
Fractions–Use figures for all numbers with
       fractions (9 3/4). Spell out and hyphenate
       common fractions used alone (three-
       quarters).
Grade 7
G7, G8 (group of countries)
Latitude, Longitude–44 degrees north, 49 degrees
       30 minutes west, etc.
Leopard 1 (tank)
line 46
9-11 (for day of terrorist attacks in United States)
1930s, '30s
       –*but* Expo 67, Expo 86 (*no apostrophe*)
1920-21, *but* 1999-2003

No. 1, number 1 (*not* number one)
page 23, p. 23
paragraph 3
Phase 2
Room 14
Round 3
Scene 3, the third scene
Section 8, Sec. 8
7Up (soft drink)
Square 1, back to
Telephone numbers–Use hyphens, not spaces or brackets to break up: 416-228-6262, 1-888-268-9237.
10 Downing Street (*exception*)
10th (*no period*)
360networks Inc.
Treaty 6
24-7 (24 hours a day, seven days a week, *but avoid*)
24 Sussex Drive (*exception*)
20th century
20th Century Fox
20-something, 30-something
two-by-four
2,4-D (weed killer)
US (used only with dollar figures: $295 US)
V-6, V-8 (engine)
verse 3

Plain Words

When there is a choice of words, prefer the short to the long, the familiar to the unfamiliar. This chapter lists some long or formal words along with some shorter or more familiar alternatives that may do the job better.

abandon	leave, quit, give up
abbreviate	shorten, cut
abduct	kidnap, seize
abolish	end, do away with, scrap
abrasion	scrape, scratch
accelerate	hurry, speed up
accessible	easily reached, ready, at hand
accommodate	house, shelter, put up
accordingly	so, therefore
according to	under; say
accumulate	pile up, collect
acknowledge	admit, concede
acquire	buy, gain, get
acquit	free, clear, release
additional	added, more, extra
in addition to	besides
adhere	stick, cling
adjacent	beside, next to, touching
administer	manage, direct, control
adverse	harmful, damaging
advise	tell, write, inform
advocate	support, call for
affluent	rich, well-to-do
aggravate	annoy, provoke, worsen
aggressive	pushing, pushy
alienate	put off, turn against
allegiance	loyalty
alleviate	ease, soften
alteration	change, revision
alternate	take turns

alternative	choice, other
amalgamate	unite, combine
amendment	change, revision
amicable	friendly, pleasant
anonymous	nameless, unknown
antagonize	offend, anger
apparent	clear, plain, obvious
appreciative	grateful, thankful
appropriate	fit, proper
approximately	about
aptitude	gift, knack, talent
arguably	perhaps, maybe
as far as...	
is concerned	as to
asphyxiate	choke, suffocate
assist	help, aid
astute	shrewd, clever
attempt	try
attired	dressed, wearing
authentic	genuine, real, true
authorize	approve, allow, give power
autonomous	free, independent, self-governing
available	ready, on hand
bargain	deal
beneficial	good for, helpful, useful
bereavement	death, loss
beverage	drink
biannual	twice a year, every two years
bigotry	bias, narrow-mindedness, racism
bilateral	two-sided
bona fide	real, in good faith
capacity	ability, position, space, size
catastrophe	disaster
cease	stop, end
censure	blame, scold
characteristic	trait, mark, feature

Plain Words

circumstance	event, condition, fact
clad	dressed, wearing
coagulate	clot, congeal
coerce	force, press
collaborate	work together, team up
comatose	unconscious
commence	begin, start
commitment	promise, pledge
communicable	catching, infectious
communicate	tell, inform, write, telephone
comparable	like, similar
compensate	pay, make up
competent	able, trained
complete	fill out, finish
complimentary	free
comply	follow, obey, give in
compulsion	urge
conceive	think up, imagine, dream up
concerning	about, for, on
conclude	end
concur	agree, match
conduct	carry on, do, run
confederation	alliance, league, union
congenital	inborn, inbred
conscientious	careful, painstaking
consequently	so
considerable	much, ample
consolation	comfort, relief, help
conspicuous	plain, obvious
constitute	are, make up, form
construct	build, make
consult	ask, talk over
consume	eat, use up
contaminate	taint, pollute, dirty, poison
contemplate	consider, study, weigh
contribute	give, share, help

controversy	debate, issue
contusion	bruise
convenient	useful, handy
convulsion	seizure, spasm
corroborate	confirm, verify
counterfeit	false, phoney, fake
courteous	polite
criterion	test, rule, model, yardstick
currently	now
deactivate	shut off, close
dearth	lack, shortage, scarcity
deceased	dead
decompose	rot, decay
decontaminate	purify, disinfect, sterilize
decrease	cut, drop, fall
decry	blame, condemn
de-emphasize	play down, softpedal
de facto	actual, real
defective	faulty, broken
deficient	lacking, poor
defraud	cheat, swindle, fleece
demonstrate	show, prove
depart	go, leave, check out
deplete	empty, sap, reduce
depreciate	lessen, cheapen, scorn
depressed	backward, diminished, sad
designate	name, call, label
destitute	poor, needy, bare
determine	fix, test, find out, decide, settle
development	growth, change
deviate	swerve, stray, turn aside, vary
dimension	size
diminutive	tiny
disallow	turn down, reject
discontinue	end, give up, stop
disembark	get off, leave, land

Plain Words

disguise	hide, mask
disintegrate	fall apart, crumble, break up
dispatch	send, issue
display	show, bare
distinguish	tell apart, make out
distribute	hand out, spread
divulge	tell, give, reveal
don	put on, get into
donation	gift, present
draconian	harsh
dubious	unsure, doubtful
duplicate	copy, repeat
dwell	live, occupy
eccentric	odd, strange
economical	thrifty, cheap
edifice	building
elevate	lift, raise
eliminate	get rid of, throw out, drop
emaciated	gaunt, bony, thin, wasted
eminent	famous, high, noted
emphasize	stress, underline
empirical	practical
employ	use, hire, apply
encounter	meet, come upon
endorsement	support, backing
enhance	add to, improve
ensue	follow, develop
enumerate	count, add up, cite
envisage	see, foresee, imagine
escalate	step up, intensify
eschew	avoid
in the event of	if
evident	plain, obvious
excessive	too much, undue
in excess of	over
exhibit	show, reveal, display

exonerate	free, clear, acquit
exorbitant	excessive, too high, overpriced
expedite	speed up, push
expenditure	spending, expense, cost
experience	feel, live through, undergo
expertise	skill, knowledge, know-how
explicit	clear, precise, exact
extended	long, drawn out
extensive	large, wide, broad, roomy
exterminate	wipe out, destroy
extinguish	put out, douse, smother
fabricate	make, build; lie, trump up
facilitate	ease, make easy, help, lighten
failed to	did not
fallacy	error, fault, pitfall
feasible	possible, can be done, workable
finalize	finish, complete, end
fluctuate	rise and fall, swing, waver
fortunate	lucky, happy
fracture	break
frequently	often
frustration	defeat, dismay
fundamental	basic, real
generate	produce, cause
gratuity	gift, tip
on the grounds that	because
hazardous	unsafe, risky, dangerous
ideology	beliefs
illumination	light, insight
illustration	example, picture, drawing
immediately	at once, now
immense	huge, vast
immovable	set, firm, fixed
impartial	neutral, fair, just
impeccable	flawless, perfect

Plain Words

impede	slow, hamper, stall, hinder
imperative	urgent, vital, pressing
imperceptible	slight, subtle, hidden
impersonate	copy, mimic
impetus	spur, push, urge
implement	do, set up, begin, carry out
impolite	rude
impostor	cheat, fraud, ringer
impotent	weak, helpless, powerless
inaccuracy	mistake, error
inadvertent	accidental, careless
inadvisable	unwise, risky
inaugurate	begin, launch
in camera	private
incapacitate	disable, damage, lay up
incarcerate	jail, intern, imprison
incision	cut, slit
incite	rouse, prod, goad
inclement	stormy, harsh, nasty
incompetent	unfit, inept
inconceivable	incredible, beyond belief
incorrect	wrong
increase	rise, go up, gain, grow
incredulous	dubious, skeptical
indefinite	vague, uncertain, dim
independent	free; well-off
indicate	show, suggest, hint, imply
indigenous	native
indignant	angry, upset
indispensable	vital, crucial, essential
individual	person, man, woman
ineligible	unfit, unsuitable
inevitable	sure, destined
inexpensive	cheap, low-priced, modest
inflexible	rigid, firm, stiff
inform	tell

ingenious	clever, deft, masterly
inherent	inborn, inbred, essential
inhibit	check, hinder, curb
initial	first
initiate	begin, open
injunction	ban, order
in lieu of	instead of
innate	inborn, natural
innovation	change, novelty
input	say, opinion, suggestion
inquire	ask
insecure	unsafe, unsure
institute	set up, begin, found
instrument	tool, agent, means
insufficient	not enough, short
insurrection	revolt, riot, mutiny
integrate	absorb, combine, mix
intention	aim, plan, goal, purpose
interface	work together, connect
intermission	pause, break
interrogate	question, pump, quiz
interrupt	break in, butt in, hinder, stop
intersection	corner
inundate	flood, deluge, overflow, engulf
irrelevant	beside the point, off-base
irresponsible	careless, rash, reckless
jurisdiction	control, power, domain
laceration	cut, tear, gash
latitude	scope, range
laud	praise
lenient	mild, gentle, sparing
liberate	free, rescue
locality	place, spot, site
locate	find, pinpoint
lubricate	oil, grease
magnitude	size, extent

Plain Words

majority	most, bulk, mass
manufacture	make, produce, build
maximum	most, biggest, longest
meaningful	big, important, significant
medication	medicine, remedy, pill, drug
mediocre	ordinary, run-of-the-mill
mentality	mind, frame of mind, outlook
methodology	method
milieu	setting, scene; culture
minimal	small, token
minimize	lessen, play down, belittle, diminish
minuscule	tiny
mitigate	ease, soften, make mild, temper
modification	change
momentous	important
motivate	inspire, drive, cause
narrate	tell, recount, relate
nauseous	sickening, repulsive
necessitate	need, compel, call for
negligent	careless
negotiate	bargain, talk business
neo-natal	newborn
neophyte	novice, beginner, learner, apprentice
neutralize	offset, cancel
nominal	small, token
notification	notice, warning
numerous	many
nurture	feed, train
nutritious	nourishing, wholesome
objective	end, aim, goal, mission
obligation	duty, debt
oblige	compel, force
obscure	dim, hidden
observation	remark, comment

obsolescent	dying out, disappearing
obsolete	worn-out, disused, out-of-date
obstruction	barrier, block, hurdle
obtain	get, come by, gain
occasion	event, cause, chance
occupation	job, trade, profession
occurrence	event, incident
ongoing	continuing, active, permanent
operate	work, run; cut out, remove
opportunity	chance
optimal	best
option	choice
originate	invent, create
outrageous	shocking, disgusting
overabundance	abundance, excess, glut
overview	view, survey
palatable	tasty, pleasing, sweet
panache	dash, pizzazz, zip
parameter	limit, boundary
paraphrase	reword, restate
parochial	narrow
participate	take part, share in, join in
pending	until, in the air
perceive	see, view, regard
periphery	edge, outskirts
permanent	lasting, endless
permission	consent, go-ahead
perquisite	perk, fringe benefit, right
persevere	persist, hold on, endure, stand
perspiration	sweat
persuade	win over, sway, coax
pertinent	fit, right, apt
philosophy	idea, view, system
physician	doctor
place	put
pollute	dirty, poison, taint

Plain Words

portion	part, piece, share
position	job
possess	own, have
postpone	put off, shelve, delay
practicable	workable, can be done
pragmatic	practical
preclude	prevent, shut out, avert
predicament	difficulty
prejudicial	harmful
preliminary to	before
preparedness	readiness
prerogative	privilege, right
presently	soon
prestigious	honoured, famous
principal	main, chief
prior to	before
probability	likelihood, chance
procedure	way, course, method
proceed	go
proficient	skilled, deft, masterly
prohibit	ban, prevent, forbid
project	plan
proliferation	spread
prophesy	foretell, predict
proponent	advocate, supporter
proposal	plan, offer
prosthesis	artificial limb
protocol	etiquette, usage
provide	give, offer, have, say
proviso	condition
provoke	stir up, annoy, tease
prowess	skill, talent
purchase	buy
for the purpose of	to
qualification	ability, skill, requirement

quandary	difficulty, impasse
radiant	bright, glowing
rampant	rife, raging, unchecked
ratification	assent, acceptance, approval
rationale	reason, thinking, theory
reciprocate	return, share
reconnaissance	survey, scrutiny
recuperate	recover, get well, rally
reduction	cut
redundant	extra, not needed
with regard to	on, about, as to
regimen	rule, system; diet
regret	be sorry
regulation	rule, law, bylaw
rehabilitate	redeem, straighten out, restore
reimburse	pay back, refund
reinforce	strengthen, brace, prop up
reiterate	repeat, say again
remainder	rest, others
remark	say
renegade	outlaw, crook, criminal
replica	copy, model
representative	agent, deputy
reprimand	rebuke, scold
repudiate	disown, reject, deny
require	need, call for, ask for
rescind	set aside, repeal, cancel
resemblance	likeness
reside	live, occupy, room
residence	house, home, apartment
respond	answer, reply
restrain	check, stop
retain	keep
retrench	cut down, reduce
retrieve	bring back, recover
reveal	show

Plain Words

rupture	break, snap
sanguine	optimistic, confident
sanitary	healthful, clean, germ-free
saturate	soak, fill, drench
segment	part
selection	choice, pick
self-confessed	confessed
significant	serious, grave
similar	like
situated	placed, put, housed
socialize	mingle, meet, make friends
solicit	ask for, beg, canvass
spacious	vast, roomy
spontaneous	unplanned, off the cuff, impulsive
state	say
stigma	stain, taint, disgrace
stimulate	arouse, stir up, excite
stringent	strict, tight
submit	give, send
subordinate	helper, assistant
subsequently	later, after that
substantiate	prove, support, back up
sufficient	enough, plenty, ample
suffocate	smother, choke
summon	send for
superficial	shallow, slight, flimsy
supersede	replace, displace
in short supply	scarce
supportive of	support
sustain	suffer, bear
syndrome	symptoms, clue
systematic	orderly, regular
technicality	detail, minor point
temperamental	moody, fickle, high-strung
terminal	fatal
terminate	end, stop

therapeutic	healing
toxic	poisonous, deadly
transform	change, alter
transmit	send
transparent	clear, lucid
traumatic	shocking
turbulent	stormy, wild, violent
ulterior	hidden
ultimate	last, final
underprivileged	poor, hard up
unfavourable	harmful, damaging, unpromising
unmistakable	clear, plain, evident
unpretentious	modest, humble
unveil	announce
updated	current
upgrade	improve, better
urbane	polished, well-bred, elegant
utilize	use
vacillate	waver, falter, hesitate
validity	truth, proof
vaunted	celebrated, famous
vehicle	car, truck, bus
velocity	speed
venue	place, site
verbatim	word for word, exactly
viable	workable, practical, usable
vicinity	near, close
visualize	see, foresee, imagine, picture
vulnerable	defenceless
withhold	hold back, refuse
withstand	bear, endure, resist, cope

Other books from The Canadian Press

The Canadian Press Stylebook

The most up-to-date and extensive style and writing guide available in Canada. The CP Stylebook is the bible consulted by journalists at Canada's national news agency as they provide thousands of words of copy each day to newspapers, television stations and radio broadcasters. It is also an indispensable guide for public relations writers, corporate communicators, civil servants and magazine editors – in fact, just about anyone looking for practical answers to questions on writing and editing. Paperback, 478 pages.

BN NewsTalk

The definitive guide to TV, radio and online journalism. If you're working in broadcast journalism, want to break into the field, or need to deal effectively with the news media, this is the book for you! Paperback, 193 pages.

Guide du journaliste

For journalists and others working in French. This is not a transalation of the CP Stylebook, but written in French, focusing on French style and writing issues. Paperback, 200 pages.

**Books can be ordered at
www.cp.org or by calling 416-507-2129**

Also from The Canadian Press

CP Command News

The only service that lets you monitor the CP Wire in real time, alerting you to "live" news stories affecting your organization, competitors and industry before they may be carried by more than 600 newspapers, radio and TV stations across Canada. Stories and event calendars from The Canadian Press can be searched, viewed and instantly e-mailed to you.

CP Wire

Real-time feed of Canadian and international news for print publications.

CP Online

Real-time feed of top Canadian and international news for websites.

CP Command News Publisher

Turnkey solution for publishing niche news online.

CP Financial Tools

Data, charts and stocks, in partnership with Stockgroup.

CP Interactive Graphics

Informative multimedia files to engage website visitors.

Broadcast News

The broadcast division of The Canadian Press provides up-to-the-minute news and information to radio and television stations, cable companies and wireless services.

CPimages

The photo division of The Canadian Press offers more than just the best pictures at your fingertips, from digital photography and photo distribution to an online picture archive.

FastChannel Network Canada

Links advertisers with thousands of newspapers, radio and TV stations across Canada and worldwide, making it possible to send or download print, audio and video ads with point-and-click ease from anywhere via the Internet.

PR Direct

The only service in Canada to automate the secure delivery of press releases, straight from your desktop to the CP Wire and directly into more than 600 editorial systems as well as to thousands of additional newsrooms across Canada. You can also send your photos directly to newsroom picture desks from coast-to-coast within seconds.

Contact us at:

www.cp.org   sales@cp.org   416-364-0321